john's
gospel

An eyewitness record of the real Jesus

www.johnsgospel.org.uk

ENGLISH STANDARD VERSION

ANGLICIZED

younglife

www.younglife.org.uk

john's gospel

This text is taken from the anglicized edition of the ESV Bible
(© 2002 HarperCollins Publishers) and is used by kind permission

Published by
Young Life (NYLC)®
Tel: 0844 884 8531
email: office@younglife.org.uk
www.younglife.org.uk
© 2021 Young Life (NYLC)®

ISBN 978-0-9576758-0-3

National Young Life Campaign Trust Ltd. Company limited by guarantee.
Registered in England & Wales No. 349294. Charity No: 207899

The Word Became Flesh

1 In the beginning was the Word, and the Word was with God, and the Word was God. ² He was in the beginning with God. ³ All things were made through him, and without him was not any thing made that was made. ⁴ In him was life, and the life was the light of men. ⁵ The light shines in the darkness, and the darkness has not overcome it.

⁶ There was a man sent from God, whose name was John. ⁷ He came as a witness, to bear witness about the light, that all might believe through him. ⁸ He was not the light, but came to bear witness about the light.

⁹ The true light, which gives light to everyone, was coming into the world. ¹⁰ He was in the world, and the world was made through him, yet the world did not know him. ¹¹ He came to his own, and his own people did not receive him. ¹² But to all who did receive him, who believed in his name, he gave the right to become children of God, ¹³ who were born, not of blood nor of the will of the flesh nor of the will of man, but of God.

¹⁴ And the Word became flesh and dwelt among us, and we have seen his glory, glory as of the only Son from the Father, full of grace and truth. ¹⁵ (John bore witness about him, and cried out, "This was he of whom I said, 'He who comes after me ranks before me, because he was before me.' ") ¹⁶ For from his fullness we have all received, grace upon grace. ¹⁷ For the law was given through Moses; grace and truth came through Jesus Christ. ¹⁸ No one has ever seen God; the only God, who is at the Father's side, he has made him known.

The Testimony of John the Baptist

¹⁹ And this is the testimony of John, when the Jews sent priests and Levites from Jerusalem to ask him,

"Who are you?" ²⁰ He confessed, and did not deny, but confessed, "I am not the Christ." ²¹ And they asked him, "What then? Are you Elijah?" He said, "I am not." "Are you the Prophet?" And he answered, "No." ²² So they said to him, "Who are you? We need to give an answer to those who sent us. What do you say about yourself?" ²³ He said, "I am the voice of one crying out in the wilderness, 'Make straight the way of the Lord', as the prophet Isaiah said."

²⁴ (Now they had been sent from the Pharisees.) ²⁵ They asked him, "Then why are you baptizing, if you are neither the Christ, nor Elijah, nor the Prophet?" ²⁶ John answered them, "I baptize with water, but among you stands one you do not know, ²⁷ even he who comes after me, the strap of whose sandal I am not worthy to untie." ²⁸ These things took place in Bethany across the Jordan, where John was baptizing.

Behold, the Lamb of God

²⁹ The next day he saw Jesus coming towards him, and said, "Behold, the Lamb of God, who takes away the sin of the world! ³⁰ This is he of whom I said, 'After me comes a man who ranks before me, because he was before me.' ³¹ I myself did not know him, but for this purpose I came baptizing with water, that he might be revealed to Israel." ³² And John bore witness: "I saw the Spirit descend from heaven like a dove, and it remained on him. ³³ I myself did not know him, but he who sent me to baptize with water said to me, 'He on whom you see the Spirit descend and remain, this is he who baptizes with the Holy Spirit.' ³⁴ And I have seen and have borne witness that this is the Son of God."

Jesus Calls the First Disciples

35 The next day again John was standing with two of his disciples, 36 and he looked at Jesus as he walked by and said, "Behold, the Lamb of God!" 37 The two disciples heard him say this, and they followed Jesus. 38 Jesus turned and saw them following and said to them, "What are you seeking?" And they said to him, "Rabbi" (which means Teacher), "where are you staying?" 39 He said to them, "Come and you will see." So they came and saw where he was staying, and they stayed with him that day, for it was about the tenth hour. 40 One of the two who heard John speak and followed Jesus was Andrew, Simon Peter's brother. 41 He first found his own brother Simon and said to him, "We have found the Messiah" (which means Christ). 42 He brought him to Jesus. Jesus looked at him and said, "You are Simon the son of John. You shall be called Cephas" (which means Peter).

Jesus Calls Philip and Nathanael

43 The next day Jesus decided to go to Galilee. He found Philip and said to him, "Follow me." 44 Now Philip was from Bethsaida, the city of Andrew and Peter. 45 Philip found Nathanael and said to him, "We have found him of whom Moses in the Law and also the prophets wrote, Jesus of Nazareth, the son of Joseph." 46 Nathanael said to him, "Can anything good come out of Nazareth?" Philip said to him, "Come and see." 47 Jesus saw Nathanael coming towards him and said of him, "Behold, an Israelite indeed, in whom there is no deceit!" 48 Nathanael said to him, "How do you know me?" Jesus answered him, "Before Philip called you, when you were under the fig tree, I saw you." 49 Nathanael answered him, "Rabbi, you are the Son of God! You are the King of Israel!" 50 Jesus answered him, "Because I said to you, 'I saw you under the fig tree',

do you believe? You will see greater things than these."
⁵¹ And he said to him, "Truly, truly, I say to you, you will see heaven opened, and the angels of God ascending and descending on the Son of Man."

Comments on Chapter 1

Some incredible statements are made here about Jesus, the central character of the Gospel of John. **Two key questions are beginning to be answered**: 'Who is this man: **what is his identity?**' and 'Why did he actually come: **what is his mission?**' The author, John (not the John mentioned in this chapter), gets straight to the point by claiming that Jesus is the Son of God himself, the creator of the world, whose mission is to deal with our biggest enemy and bring us into a personal relationship with God. This promises to be some book!

Think it through

1. John's Gospel presents Jesus as a unique man, standing out from the rest of humanity. Do you think there are any grounds for this claim?

2. If Jesus really is the Son of God, there are big implications for us today. How willing are you for his life to impact yours?

watch video clip
www.johnsgospel.org.uk/chapter1

Notes:

v1 and v14: 'the Word' is a name given to Jesus ('v' refers to the verse number – see the small numbers within the chapter)

The Wedding at Cana

2 On the third day there was a wedding at Cana in Galilee, and the mother of Jesus was there. [2] Jesus also was invited to the wedding with his disciples. [3] When the wine ran out, the mother of Jesus said to him, "They have no wine." [4] And Jesus said to her, "Woman, what does this have to do with me? My hour has not yet come." [5] His mother said to the servants, "Do whatever he tells you."

[6] Now there were six stone water jars there for the Jewish rites of purification, each holding twenty or thirty gallons. [7] Jesus said to the servants, "Fill the jars with water." And they filled them up to the brim. [8] And he said to them, "Now draw some out and take it to the master of the feast." So they took it. [9] When the master of the feast tasted the water now become wine, and did not know where it came from (though the servants who had drawn the water knew), the master of the feast called the bridegroom [10] and said to him, "Everyone serves the good wine first, and when people have drunk freely, then the poor wine. But you have kept the good wine until now." [11] This, the first of his signs, Jesus did at Cana in Galilee, and manifested his glory. And his disciples believed in him.

[12] After this he went down to Capernaum, with his mother and his brothers and his disciples, and they stayed there for a few days.

Jesus Cleanses the Temple

[13] The Passover of the Jews was at hand, and Jesus went up to Jerusalem. [14] In the temple he found those who were selling oxen and sheep and pigeons, and the money-changers sitting there. [15] And making a whip of cords, he drove them all out of the temple, with the sheep and oxen. And he poured out the coins of the

money-changers and overturned their tables. ¹⁶ And he told those who sold the pigeons, "Take these things away; do not make my Father's house a house of trade." ¹⁷ His disciples remembered that it was written, "Zeal for your house will consume me."

¹⁸ So the Jews said to him, "What sign do you show us for doing these things?" ¹⁹ Jesus answered them, "Destroy this temple, and in three days I will raise it up." ²⁰ The Jews then said, "It has taken forty-six years to build this temple, and will you raise it up in three days?" ²¹ But he was speaking about the temple of his body. ²² When therefore he was raised from the dead, his disciples remembered that he had said this, and they believed the Scripture and the word that Jesus had spoken.

Jesus Knows What Is in Man

²³ Now when he was in Jerusalem at the Passover Feast, many believed in his name when they saw the signs that he was doing. ²⁴ But Jesus on his part did not entrust himself to them, because he knew all people ²⁵ and needed no one to bear witness about man, for he himself knew what was in man.

Comments on Chapter 2

Anyone can make the claim of being God, but if it's true, there needs to be evidence to back it up. Jesus starts to prove that he really is who he says he is and that he does have the authority to complete what he has come to do. Who else could turn water into wine, fulfil predictions made hundreds of years earlier, and even foretell his own death and subsequent coming back to life again?

Think it through

1. These signs are done to give people strong evidence to help them believe – and many do here! How do you explain these signs?
2. It isn't just Jesus' keen followers who believe (v23). Are you genuinely willing to go wherever the evidence leads?

watch video clip
www.johnsgospel.org.uk/chapter2

You Must Be Born Again

3 Now there was a man of the Pharisees named Nicodemus, a ruler of the Jews. ² This man came to Jesus by night and said to him, "Rabbi, we know that you are a teacher come from God, for no one can do these signs that you do unless God is with him." ³ Jesus answered him, "Truly, truly, I say to you, unless one is born again he cannot see the kingdom of God." ⁴ Nicodemus said to him, "How can a man be born when he is old? Can he enter a second time into his mother's womb and be born?" ⁵ Jesus answered, "Truly, truly, I say to you, unless one is born of water and the Spirit, he cannot enter the kingdom of God. ⁶ That which is born of the flesh is flesh, and that which is born of the Spirit is spirit. ⁷ Do not marvel that I said to you, 'You must be born again.' ⁸ The wind blows where it wishes, and you hear its sound, but you do not know where it comes from or where it goes. So it is with everyone who is born of the Spirit."

⁹ Nicodemus said to him, "How can these things be?" ¹⁰ Jesus answered him, "Are you the teacher of Israel and yet you do not understand these things? ¹¹ Truly, truly, I say to you, we speak of what we know, and bear witness to what we have seen, but you do not receive our testimony. ¹² If I have told you earthly things and you do not believe, how can you believe if I tell you heavenly things? ¹³ No one has ascended into heaven except he who descended from heaven, the Son of Man. ¹⁴ And as Moses lifted up the serpent in the wilderness, so must the Son of Man be lifted up, ¹⁵ that whoever believes in him may have eternal life.

For God So Loved the World

¹⁶ "For God so loved the world, that he gave his only Son, that whoever believes in him should not perish but

have eternal life. ¹⁷ For God did not send his Son into the world to condemn the world, but in order that the world might be saved through him. ¹⁸ Whoever believes in him is not condemned, but whoever does not believe is condemned already, because he has not believed in the name of the only Son of God. ¹⁹ And this is the judgement: the light has come into the world, and people loved the darkness rather than the light because their works were evil. ²⁰ For everyone who does wicked things hates the light and does not come to the light, lest his works should be exposed. ²¹ But whoever does what is true comes to the light, so that it may be clearly seen that his works have been carried out in God."

John the Baptist Exalts Christ

²² After this Jesus and his disciples went into the Judean countryside, and he remained there with them and was baptizing. ²³ John also was baptizing at Aenon near Salim, because water was plentiful there, and people were coming and being baptized ²⁴ (for John had not yet been put in prison).

²⁵ Now a discussion arose between some of John's disciples and a Jew over purification. ²⁶ And they came to John and said to him, "Rabbi, he who was with you across the Jordan, to whom you bore witness—look, he is baptizing, and all are going to him." ²⁷ John answered, "A person cannot receive even one thing unless it is given him from heaven. ²⁸ You yourselves bear me witness, that I said, 'I am not the Christ, but I have been sent before him.' ²⁹ The one who has the bride is the bridegroom. The friend of the bridegroom, who stands and hears him, rejoices greatly at the bridegroom's voice. Therefore this joy of mine is now complete. ³⁰ He must increase, but I must decrease."

³¹ He who comes from above is above all. He who is of the earth belongs to the earth and speaks in an earthly way. He who comes from heaven is above all. ³² He bears witness to what he has seen and heard, yet no one receives his testimony. ³³ Whoever receives his testimony sets his seal to this, that God is true. ³⁴ For he whom God has sent utters the words of God, for he gives the Spirit without measure. ³⁵ The Father loves the Son and has given all things into his hand. ³⁶ Whoever believes in the Son has eternal life; whoever does not obey the Son shall not see life, but the wrath of God remains on him.

Comments on Chapter 3

More is unpacked for us in this chapter about why Jesus came. It's all to do with our ultimate destiny; it affects you! Jesus sets out our two options: it's either **eternal life** or **condemnation and wrath** – or in other words, heaven or hell. The deciding factor is whether you believe and trust in Jesus or not (v16, v36). Heaven isn't our default destiny! See why it's so crucial? Spoiler alert: the whole reason Jesus came was to make eternal life possible for you, to make it your destiny.

Think it through

1. Do you agree with Jesus' statement that people naturally love darkness rather than light, sin rather than purity (v19–20)? How would you justify your answer?
2. How do you think Jesus' statement applies to you? Do you have a natural tendency to sin?

.watch video clip
www.johnsgospel.org.uk/chapter3

Notes:

John 3:16 is probably the best-known verse in the whole Bible!

Jesus and the Woman of Samaria

4 Now when Jesus learned that the Pharisees had heard that Jesus was making and baptizing more disciples than John ² (although Jesus himself did not baptize, but only his disciples), ³ he left Judea and departed again for Galilee. ⁴ And he had to pass through Samaria. ⁵ So he came to a town of Samaria called Sychar, near the field that Jacob had given to his son Joseph. ⁶ Jacob's well was there; so Jesus, wearied as he was from his journey, was sitting beside the well. It was about the sixth hour.

⁷ A woman from Samaria came to draw water. Jesus said to her, "Give me a drink." ⁸ (For his disciples had gone away into the city to buy food.) ⁹ The Samaritan woman said to him, "How is it that you, a Jew, ask for a drink from me, a woman of Samaria?" (For Jews have no dealings with Samaritans.) ¹⁰ Jesus answered her, "If you knew the gift of God, and who it is that is saying to you, 'Give me a drink', you would have asked him, and he would have given you living water." ¹¹ The woman said to him, "Sir, you have nothing to draw water with, and the well is deep. Where do you get that living water? ¹² Are you greater than our father Jacob? He gave us the well and drank from it himself, as did his sons and his livestock." ¹³ Jesus said to her, "Everyone who drinks of this water will be thirsty again, ¹⁴ but whoever drinks of the water that I will give him will never be thirsty again. The water that I will give him will become in him a spring of water welling up to eternal life." ¹⁵ The woman said to him, "Sir, give me this water, so that I will not be thirsty or have to come here to draw water."

¹⁶ Jesus said to her, "Go, call your husband, and come here." ¹⁷ The woman answered him, "I have no husband." Jesus said to her, "You are right in saying, 'I have no husband'; ¹⁸ for you have had five husbands, and the one

you now have is not your husband. What you have said is true." 19 The woman said to him, "Sir, I perceive that you are a prophet. 20 Our fathers worshipped on this mountain, but you say that in Jerusalem is the place where people ought to worship." 21 Jesus said to her, "Woman, believe me, the hour is coming when neither on this mountain nor in Jerusalem will you worship the Father. 22 You worship what you do not know; we worship what we know, for salvation is from the Jews. 23 But the hour is coming, and is now here, when the true worshippers will worship the Father in spirit and truth, for the Father is seeking such people to worship him. 24 God is spirit, and those who worship him must worship in spirit and truth." 25 The woman said to him, "I know that Messiah is coming (he who is called Christ). When he comes, he will tell us all things." 26 Jesus said to her, "I who speak to you am he."

27 Just then his disciples came back. They marvelled that he was talking with a woman, but no one said, "What do you seek?" or, "Why are you talking with her?" 28 So the woman left her water jar and went away into town and said to the people, 29 "Come, see a man who told me all that I ever did. Can this be the Christ?" 30 They went out of the town and were coming to him.

31 Meanwhile the disciples were urging him, saying, "Rabbi, eat." 32 But he said to them, "I have food to eat that you do not know about." 33 So the disciples said to one another, "Has anyone brought him something to eat?" 34 Jesus said to them, "My food is to do the will of him who sent me and to accomplish his work. 35 Do you not say, 'There are yet four months, then comes the harvest'? Look, I tell you, lift up your eyes, and see that the fields are white for harvest. 36 Already the one who reaps is receiving wages and gathering fruit for eternal life, so that sower and reaper may rejoice together. 37 For here the saying holds

true, 'One sows and another reaps.' 38 I sent you to reap that for which you did not labour. Others have laboured, and you have entered into their labour."

39 Many Samaritans from that town believed in him because of the woman's testimony, "He told me all that I ever did." 40 So when the Samaritans came to him, they asked him to stay with them, and he stayed there two days. 41 And many more believed because of his word. 42 They said to the woman, "It is no longer because of what you said that we believe, for we have heard for ourselves, and we know that this is indeed the Saviour of the world."

43 After the two days he departed for Galilee. 44 (For Jesus himself had testified that a prophet has no honour in his own home town.) 45 So when he came to Galilee, the Galileans welcomed him, having seen all that he had done in Jerusalem at the feast. For they too had gone to the feast.

Jesus Heals an Official's Son

46 So he came again to Cana in Galilee, where he had made the water wine. And at Capernaum there was an official whose son was ill. 47 When this man heard that Jesus had come from Judea to Galilee, he went to him and asked him to come down and heal his son, for he was at the point of death. 48 So Jesus said to him, "Unless you see signs and wonders you will not believe." 49 The official said to him, "Sir, come down before my child dies." 50 Jesus said to him, "Go; your son will live." The man believed the word that Jesus spoke to him and went on his way. 51 As he was going down, his servants met him and told him that his son was recovering. 52 So he asked them the hour when he began to get better, and they said to him, "Yesterday at the seventh hour the fever left him." 53 The father knew that was the hour when Jesus had said

to him, "Your son will live." And he himself believed, and all his household. [54] This was now the second sign that Jesus did when he had come from Judea to Galilee.

Comments on Chapter 4

At first the Samaritan woman doesn't have a clue who Jesus really is! Although their conversation is uncomfortable and humbling for her, she slowly becomes convinced of Jesus' true identity. In the same way, the people of her city, once they see Jesus, also believe that he really is the Christ, the Saviour of the world. But the nobleman is different – he believes even before he sees!

Think it through

1. The woman is convinced that Jesus has come from God when Jesus tells her details he couldn't possibly have known were he just a normal man. If you were in the woman's shoes, do you think you'd have been convinced?

2. How does it make you feel to think that God knows details about you that you would rather keep secret?

3. Jesus offers the woman true life. Are you, like her, dissatisfied with how unfulfilling life is at times?

watch video clip
www.johnsgospel.org.uk/chapter4

The Healing at the Pool on the Sabbath

5 After this there was a feast of the Jews, and Jesus went up to Jerusalem.

2 Now there is in Jerusalem by the Sheep Gate a pool, in Aramaic called Bethesda, which has five roofed colonnades. 3 In these lay a multitude of invalids— blind, lame, and paralysed. 5 One man was there who had been an invalid for thirty-eight years. 6 When Jesus saw him lying there and knew that he had already been there a long time, he said to him, "Do you want to be healed?" 7 The sick man answered him, "Sir, I have no one to put me into the pool when the water is stirred up, and while I am going another steps down before me." 8 Jesus said to him, "Get up, take up your bed, and walk." 9 And at once the man was healed, and he took up his bed and walked.

Now that day was the Sabbath. 10 So the Jews said to the man who had been healed, "It is the Sabbath, and it is not lawful for you to take up your bed." 11 But he answered them, "The man who healed me, that man said to me, 'Take up your bed, and walk.'" 12 They asked him, "Who is the man who said to you, 'Take up your bed and walk'?" 13 Now the man who had been healed did not know who it was, for Jesus had withdrawn, as there was a crowd in the place. 14 Afterwards Jesus found him in the temple and said to him, "See, you are well! Sin no more, that nothing worse may happen to you." 15 The man went away and told the Jews that it was Jesus who had healed him. 16 And this was why the Jews were persecuting Jesus, because he was doing these things on the Sabbath. 17 But Jesus answered them, "My Father is working until now, and I am working."

Jesus Is Equal with God

18 This was why the Jews were seeking all the more to

kill him, because not only was he breaking the Sabbath, but he was even calling God his own Father, making himself equal with God.

The Authority of the Son

¹⁹ So Jesus said to them, "Truly, truly, I say to you, the Son can do nothing of his own accord, but only what he sees the Father doing. For whatever the Father does, that the Son does likewise. ²⁰ For the Father loves the Son and shows him all that he himself is doing. And greater works than these will he show him, so that you may marvel. ²¹ For as the Father raises the dead and gives them life, so also the Son gives life to whom he will. ²² The Father judges no one, but has given all judgement to the Son, ²³ that all may honour the Son, just as they honour the Father. Whoever does not honour the Son does not honour the Father who sent him. ²⁴ Truly, truly, I say to you, whoever hears my word and believes him who sent me has eternal life. He does not come into judgement, but has passed from death to life.

²⁵ "Truly, truly, I say to you, an hour is coming, and is now here, when the dead will hear the voice of the Son of God, and those who hear will live. ²⁶ For as the Father has life in himself, so he has granted the Son also to have life in himself. ²⁷ And he has given him authority to execute judgement, because he is the Son of Man. ²⁸ Do not marvel at this, for an hour is coming when all who are in the tombs will hear his voice ²⁹ and come out, those who have done good to the resurrection of life, and those who have done evil to the resurrection of judgement.

Witnesses to Jesus

³⁰ "I can do nothing on my own. As I hear, I judge, and my judgement is just, because I seek not my own will but

the will of him who sent me. ³¹ If I alone bear witness about myself, my testimony is not true. ³² There is another who bears witness about me, and I know that the testimony that he bears about me is true. ³³ You sent to John, and he has borne witness to the truth. ³⁴ Not that the testimony that I receive is from man, but I say these things so that you may be saved. ³⁵ He was a burning and shining lamp, and you were willing to rejoice for a while in his light. ³⁶ But the testimony that I have is greater than that of John. For the works that the Father has given me to accomplish, the very works that I am doing, bear witness about me that the Father has sent me. ³⁷ And the Father who sent me has himself borne witness about me. His voice you have never heard, his form you have never seen, ³⁸ and you do not have his word abiding in you, for you do not believe the one whom he has sent. ³⁹ You search the Scriptures because you think that in them you have eternal life; and it is they that bear witness about me, ⁴⁰ yet you refuse to come to me that you may have life. ⁴¹ I do not receive glory from people. ⁴² But I know that you do not have the love of God within you. ⁴³ I have come in my Father's name, and you do not receive me. If another comes in his own name, you will receive him. ⁴⁴ How can you believe, when you receive glory from one another and do not seek the glory that comes from the only God? ⁴⁵ Do not think that I will accuse you to the Father. There is one who accuses you: Moses, on whom you have set your hope. ⁴⁶ For if you believed Moses, you would believe me; for he wrote of me. ⁴⁷ But if you do not believe his writings, how will you believe my words?"

Comments on Chapter 5

Not everyone believes… especially the religious leaders! They hate Jesus, and even want to kill him – but why? He shows them up for what they really are: hypocrites with strict rules, but devoid of any true relationship with God. Jesus doesn't conform to their rules, nor does he conform to their warped idea of God – and so they reject him. How tragic – they could have life, if only they would come to him (v40).

Think it through

1. Why do you think religious people often find it hard to admit their wrongdoing and come to Jesus?
2. Do you think that living a moral life will make you more acceptable to God?

watch video clip
www.johnsgospel.org.uk/chapter5

Jesus Feeds the Five Thousand

6 After this Jesus went away to the other side of the Sea of Galilee, which is the Sea of Tiberias. ² And a large crowd was following him, because they saw the signs that he was doing on the sick. ³ Jesus went up on the mountain, and there he sat down with his disciples. ⁴ Now the Passover, the feast of the Jews, was at hand. ⁵ Lifting up his eyes, then, and seeing that a large crowd was coming towards him, Jesus said to Philip, "Where are we to buy bread, so that these people may eat?" ⁶ He said this to test him, for he himself knew what he would do. ⁷ Philip answered him, "Two hundred denarii worth of bread would not be enough for each of them to get a little." ⁸ One of his disciples, Andrew, Simon Peter's brother, said to him, ⁹ "There is a boy here who has five barley loaves and two fish, but what are they for so many?" ¹⁰ Jesus said, "Make the people sit down." Now there was much grass in the place. So the men sat down, about five thousand in number. ¹¹ Jesus then took the loaves, and when he had given thanks, he distributed them to those who were seated. So also the fish, as much as they wanted. ¹² And when they had eaten their fill, he told his disciples, "Gather up the leftover fragments, that nothing may be lost." ¹³ So they gathered them up and filled twelve baskets with fragments from the five barley loaves left by those who had eaten. ¹⁴ When the people saw the sign that he had done, they said, "This is indeed the Prophet who is to come into the world!"

¹⁵ Perceiving then that they were about to come and take him by force to make him king, Jesus withdrew again to the mountain by himself.

Jesus Walks on Water

¹⁶ When evening came, his disciples went down to the

lake, ¹⁷ got into a boat, and started across the lake to Capernaum. It was now dark, and Jesus had not yet come to them. ¹⁸ The lake became rough because a strong wind was blowing. ¹⁹ When they had rowed about three or four miles, they saw Jesus walking on the lake and coming near the boat, and they were frightened. ²⁰ But he said to them, "It is I; do not be afraid." ²¹ Then they were glad to take him into the boat, and immediately the boat was at the land to which they were going.

I Am the Bread of Life

²² On the next day the crowd that remained on the other side of the lake saw that there had been only one boat there, and that Jesus had not entered the boat with his disciples, but that his disciples had gone away alone. ²³ Other boats from Tiberias came near the place where they had eaten the bread after the Lord had given thanks. ²⁴ So when the crowd saw that Jesus was not there, nor his disciples, they themselves got into the boats and went to Capernaum, seeking Jesus.

²⁵ When they found him on the other side of the lake, they said to him, "Rabbi, when did you come here?" ²⁶ Jesus answered them, "Truly, truly, I say to you, you are seeking me, not because you saw signs, but because you ate your fill of the loaves. ²⁷ Do not work for the food that perishes, but for the food that endures to eternal life, which the Son of Man will give to you. For on him God the Father has set his seal." ²⁸ Then they said to him, "What must we do, to be doing the works of God?" ²⁹ Jesus answered them, "This is the work of God, that you believe in him whom he has sent." ³⁰ So they said to him, "Then what sign do you do, that we may see and believe you? What work do you perform? ³¹ Our fathers ate the manna in the wilderness; as it is written, 'He gave them bread from heaven to eat.'"

³² Jesus then said to them, "Truly, truly, I say to you, it was not Moses who gave you the bread from heaven, but my Father gives you the true bread from heaven. ³³ For the bread of God is he who comes down from heaven and gives life to the world." ³⁴ They said to him, "Sir, give us this bread always."

³⁵ Jesus said to them, "I am the bread of life; whoever comes to me shall not hunger, and whoever believes in me shall never thirst. ³⁶ But I said to you that you have seen me and yet do not believe. ³⁷ All that the Father gives me will come to me, and whoever comes to me I will never cast out. ³⁸ For I have come down from heaven, not to do my own will but the will of him who sent me. ³⁹ And this is the will of him who sent me, that I should lose nothing of all that he has given me, but raise it up on the last day. ⁴⁰ For this is the will of my Father, that everyone who looks on the Son and believes in him should have eternal life, and I will raise him up on the last day."

⁴¹ So the Jews grumbled about him, because he said, "I am the bread that came down from heaven." ⁴² They said, "Is not this Jesus, the son of Joseph, whose father and mother we know? How does he now say, 'I have come down from heaven'?" ⁴³ Jesus answered them, "Do not grumble among yourselves. ⁴⁴ No one can come to me unless the Father who sent me draws him. And I will raise him up on the last day. ⁴⁵ It is written in the Prophets, 'And they will all be taught by God.' Everyone who has heard and learned from the Father comes to me— ⁴⁶ not that anyone has seen the Father except he who is from God; he has seen the Father. ⁴⁷ Truly, truly, I say to you, whoever believes has eternal life. ⁴⁸ I am the bread of life. ⁴⁹ Your fathers ate the manna in the wilderness, and they died. ⁵⁰ This is the bread that comes down from heaven, so that one may eat of it and not die. ⁵¹ I am the living bread that

came down from heaven. If anyone eats of this bread, he will live for ever. And the bread that I will give for the life of the world is my flesh."

⁵² The Jews then disputed among themselves, saying, "How can this man give us his flesh to eat?" ⁵³ So Jesus said to them, "Truly, truly, I say to you, unless you eat the flesh of the Son of Man and drink his blood, you have no life in you. ⁵⁴ Whoever feeds on my flesh and drinks my blood has eternal life, and I will raise him up on the last day. ⁵⁵ For my flesh is true food, and my blood is true drink. ⁵⁶ Whoever feeds on my flesh and drinks my blood abides in me, and I in him. ⁵⁷ As the living Father sent me, and I live because of the Father, so whoever feeds on me, he also will live because of me. ⁵⁸ This is the bread that came down from heaven, not like the bread the fathers ate, and died. Whoever feeds on this bread will live forever." ⁵⁹ Jesus said these things in the synagogue, as he taught at Capernaum.

The Words of Eternal Life

⁶⁰ When many of his disciples heard it, they said, "This is a hard saying; who can listen to it?" ⁶¹ But Jesus, knowing in himself that his disciples were grumbling about this, said to them, "Do you take offence at this? ⁶² Then what if you were to see the Son of Man ascending to where he was before? ⁶³ It is the Spirit who gives life; the flesh is no help at all. The words that I have spoken to you are spirit and life. ⁶⁴ But there are some of you who do not believe." (For Jesus knew from the beginning who those were who did not believe, and who it was who would betray him.) ⁶⁵ And he said, "This is why I told you that no one can come to me unless it is granted him by the Father."

⁶⁶ After this many of his disciples turned back and no longer walked with him. ⁶⁷ So Jesus said to the Twelve,

"Do you want to go away as well?" [68] Simon Peter answered him, "Lord, to whom shall we go? You have the words of eternal life, [69] and we have believed, and have come to know, that you are the Holy One of God." [70] Jesus answered them, "Did I not choose you, the Twelve? And yet one of you is a devil." [71] He spoke of Judas the son of Simon Iscariot, for he, one of the Twelve, was going to betray him.

Comments on Chapter 6.

Yet again, Jesus is totally misunderstood. One moment the people want to make him king, the next they're offended and leave. The problem is that they are consumed with the here and now – sound familiar? But Jesus makes an important distinction between the **temporal** and the **eternal**. Yes, he can provide for physical needs, but it was to give eternal life that he came.

Think it through

1. We look for satisfaction in life in so many different ways, but as with eating, it's not long till we are hungry and dissatisfied again. In what areas can you see this in your life?

2. Philip can't imagine how they are possibly going to feed all these people; he doesn't think Jesus has the power to solve the problem. What issues do you have in your life that you think are just too big for Jesus to be able to deal with?

watch video clip

www.johnsgospel.org.uk/chapter6

Notes:

v53–58: Jesus is not promoting cannibalism! He is talking about a spiritual truth, not a literal action. He is saying: 'Just as you take food and drink within your body and it becomes part of you, so you must receive me within your innermost being so that I can give you life.'

Jesus at the Feast of Booths

7 After this Jesus went about in Galilee. He would not go about in Judea, because the Jews were seeking to kill him. 2 Now the Jews' Feast of Booths was at hand. 3 So his brothers said to him, "Leave here and go to Judea, that your disciples also may see the works you are doing. 4 For no one works in secret if he seeks to be known openly. If you do these things, show yourself to the world." 5 For not even his brothers believed in him. 6 Jesus said to them, "My time has not yet come, but your time is always here. 7 The world cannot hate you, but it hates me because I testify about it that its works are evil. 8 You go up to the feast. I am not going up to this feast, for my time has not yet fully come." 9 After saying this, he remained in Galilee.

10 But after his brothers had gone up to the feast, then he also went up, not publicly but in private. 11 The Jews were looking for him at the feast, and saying, "Where is he?" 12 And there was much muttering about him among the people. While some said, "He is a good man", others said, "No, he is leading the people astray." 13 Yet for fear of the Jews no one spoke openly of him.

14 About the middle of the feast Jesus went up into the temple and began teaching. 15 The Jews therefore marvelled, saying, "How is it that this man has learning, when he has never studied?" 16 So Jesus answered them, "My teaching is not mine, but his who sent me. 17 If anyone's will is to do God's will, he will know whether the teaching is from God or whether I am speaking on my own authority. 18 The one who speaks on his own authority seeks his own glory; but the one who seeks the glory of him who sent him is true, and in him there is no falsehood. 19 Has not Moses given you the law? Yet none of you keeps the law. Why do you seek to kill me?" 20 The crowd answered,

"You have a demon! Who is seeking to kill you?" 21 Jesus answered them, "I did one work, and you all marvel at it. 22 Moses gave you circumcision (not that it is from Moses, but from the fathers), and you circumcise a man on the Sabbath. 23 If on the Sabbath a man receives circumcision, so that the law of Moses may not be broken, are you angry with me because on the Sabbath I made a man's whole body well? 24 Do not judge by appearances, but judge with right judgement."

Can This Be the Christ?

25 Some of the people of Jerusalem therefore said, "Is not this the man whom they seek to kill? 26 And here he is, speaking openly, and they say nothing to him! Can it be that the authorities really know that this is the Christ? 27 But we know where this man comes from, and when the Christ appears, no one will know where he comes from." 28 So Jesus proclaimed, as he taught in the temple, "You know me, and you know where I come from. But I have not come of my own accord. He who sent me is true, and him you do not know. 29 I know him, for I come from him, and he sent me." 30 So they were seeking to arrest him, but no one laid a hand on him, because his hour had not yet come. 31 Yet many of the people believed in him. They said, "When the Christ appears, will he do more signs than this man has done?"

Officers Sent to Arrest Jesus

32 The Pharisees heard the crowd muttering these things about him, and the chief priests and Pharisees sent officers to arrest him. 33 Jesus then said, "I will be with you a little longer, and then I am going to him who sent me. 34 You will seek me and you will not find me. Where I am you cannot come." 35 The Jews said to one another,

"Where does this man intend to go that we will not find him? Does he intend to go to the Dispersion among the Greeks and teach the Greeks? 36 What does he mean by saying, 'You will seek me and you will not find me', and, 'Where I am you cannot come'?"

Rivers of Living Water

37 On the last day of the feast, the great day, Jesus stood up and cried out, "If anyone thirsts, let him come to me and drink. 38 Whoever believes in me, as the Scripture has said, 'Out of his heart will flow rivers of living water.' " 39 Now this he said about the Spirit, whom those who believed in him were to receive, for as yet the Spirit had not been given, because Jesus was not yet glorified.

Division Among the People

40 When they heard these words, some of the people said, "This really is the Prophet." 41 Others said, "This is the Christ." But some said, "Is the Christ to come from Galilee? 42 Has not the Scripture said that the Christ comes from the offspring of David, and comes from Bethlehem, the village where David was?" 43 So there was a division among the people over him. 44 Some of them wanted to arrest him, but no one laid hands on him.

45 The officers then came to the chief priests and Pharisees, who said to them, "Why did you not bring him?" 46 The officers answered, "No one ever spoke like this man!" 47 The Pharisees answered them, "Have you also been deceived? 48 Have any of the authorities or the Pharisees believed in him? 49 But this crowd that does not know the law is accursed." 50 Nicodemus, who had gone to him before, and who was one of them, said to them, 51 "Does our law judge a man without first giving him a hearing and learning what he does?" 52 They replied, "Are

you from Galilee too? Search and see that no prophet arises from Galilee."

⁵³ They went each to his own house.

Comments on Chapter 7

Identity crisis! Opinion today remains just as divided as to who Jesus really is. Is he a good man, a bad man, or the Son of God? All these views are expressed in this chapter. The evidence as to his true identity is becoming harder to deny and the religious leaders know it – but they're in open denial. They hate Jesus for exposing their own hypocrisy, and brand anyone who believes him to be God as ignorant.

Think it through

1. Who do you think Jesus really is? Is your opinion starting to change?
2. The constantly recurring theme of Jesus' teaching is his ability and willingness to give **life** (described here as 'rivers of living water') – a new type of life that is so rich and full, it's unlike anything else in this world! To have this life, you first have to admit you are thirsty and in need. What do you think this involves, and why is it so hard to do?

watch video clip
www.johnsgospel.org.uk/chapter7

The Woman Caught in Adultery

8 But Jesus went to the Mount of Olives. 2 Early in the morning he came again to the temple. All the people came to him, and he sat down and taught them. 3 The scribes and the Pharisees brought a woman who had been caught in adultery, and placing her in the midst 4 they said to him, "Teacher, this woman has been caught in the act of adultery. 5 Now in the Law Moses commanded us to stone such women. So what do you say?" 6 This they said to test him, that they might have some charge to bring against him. Jesus bent down and wrote with his finger on the ground. 7 And as they continued to ask him, he stood up and said to them, "Let him who is without sin among you be the first to throw a stone at her." 8 And once more he bent down and wrote on the ground. 9 But when they heard it, they went away one by one, beginning with the older ones, and Jesus was left alone with the woman standing before him. 10 Jesus stood up and said to her, "Woman, where are they? Has no one condemned you?" 11 She said, "No one, Lord." And Jesus said, "Neither do I condemn you; go, and from now on sin no more."

I Am the Light of the World

12 Again Jesus spoke to them, saying, "I am the light of the world. Whoever follows me will not walk in darkness, but will have the light of life." 13 So the Pharisees said to him, "You are bearing witness about yourself; your testimony is not true." 14 Jesus answered, "Even if I do bear witness about myself, my testimony is true, for I know where I came from and where I am going, but you do not know where I come from or where I am going. 15 You judge according to the flesh; I judge no one. 16 Yet even if I do judge, my judgement is true, for it is not I alone

who judge, but I and the Father who sent me. ¹⁷ In your Law it is written that the testimony of two people is true. ¹⁸ I am the one who bears witness about myself, and the Father who sent me bears witness about me." ¹⁹ They said to him therefore, "Where is your Father?" Jesus answered, "You know neither me nor my Father. If you knew me, you would know my Father also." ²⁰ These words he spoke in the treasury, as he taught in the temple; but no one arrested him, because his hour had not yet come.

²¹ So he said to them again, "I am going away, and you will seek me, and you will die in your sin. Where I am going, you cannot come." ²² So the Jews said, "Will he kill himself, since he says, 'Where I am going, you cannot come'?" ²³ He said to them, "You are from below; I am from above. You are of this world; I am not of this world. ²⁴ I told you that you would die in your sins, for unless you believe that I am he you will die in your sins." ²⁵ So they said to him, "Who are you?" Jesus said to them, "Just what I have been telling you from the beginning. ²⁶ I have much to say about you and much to judge, but he who sent me is true, and I declare to the world what I have heard from him." ²⁷ They did not understand that he had been speaking to them about the Father. ²⁸ So Jesus said to them, "When you have lifted up the Son of Man, then you will know that I am he, and that I do nothing on my own authority, but speak just as the Father taught me. ²⁹ And he who sent me is with me. He has not left me alone, for I always do the things that are pleasing to him." ³⁰ As he was saying these things, many believed in him.

The Truth Will Set You Free

³¹ So Jesus said to the Jews who had believed him, "If you abide in my word, you are truly my disciples, ³² and you will know the truth, and the truth will set you free."

³³ They answered him, "We are offspring of Abraham and have never been enslaved to anyone. How is it that you say, 'You will become free'?"

³⁴ Jesus answered them, "Truly, truly, I say to you, everyone who practises sin is a slave to sin. ³⁵ The slave does not remain in the house for ever; the son remains for ever. ³⁶ So if the Son sets you free, you will be free indeed. ³⁷ I know that you are offspring of Abraham; yet you seek to kill me because my word finds no place in you. ³⁸ I speak of what I have seen with my Father, and you do what you have heard from your father."

You Are of Your Father the Devil

³⁹ They answered him, "Abraham is our father." Jesus said to them, "If you were Abraham's children, you would be doing the works Abraham did, ⁴⁰ but now you seek to kill me, a man who has told you the truth that I heard from God. This is not what Abraham did. ⁴¹ You are doing the works your father did." They said to him, "We were not born of sexual immorality. We have one Father—even God." ⁴² Jesus said to them, "If God were your Father, you would love me, for I came from God and I am here. I came not of my own accord, but he sent me. ⁴³ Why do you not understand what I say? It is because you cannot bear to hear my word. ⁴⁴ You are of your father the devil, and your will is to do your father's desires. He was a murderer from the beginning, and does not stand in the truth, because there is no truth in him. When he lies, he speaks out of his own character, for he is a liar and the father of lies. ⁴⁵ But because I tell the truth, you do not believe me. ⁴⁶ Which one of you convicts me of sin? If I tell the truth, why do you not believe me? ⁴⁷ Whoever is of God hears the words of God. The reason why you do not hear them is that you are not of God."

Before Abraham Was, I Am

[48] The Jews answered him, "Are we not right in saying that you are a Samaritan and have a demon?" [49] Jesus answered, "I do not have a demon, but I honour my Father, and you dishonour me. [50] Yet I do not seek my own glory; there is One who seeks it, and he is the judge. [51] Truly, truly, I say to you, if anyone keeps my word, he will never see death." [52] The Jews said to him, "Now we know that you have a demon! Abraham died, as did the prophets, yet you say, 'If anyone keeps my word, he will never taste death.' [53] Are you greater than our father Abraham, who died? And the prophets died! Who do you make yourself out to be?" [54] Jesus answered, "If I glorify myself, my glory is nothing. It is my Father who glorifies me, of whom you say, 'He is our God.' [55] But you have not known him. I know him. If I were to say that I do not know him, I would be a liar like you, but I do know him and I keep his word. [56] Your father Abraham rejoiced that he would see my day. He saw it and was glad." [57] So the Jews said to him, "You are not yet fifty years old, and have you seen Abraham?" [58] Jesus said to them, "Truly, truly, I say to you, before Abraham was, I am." [59] So they picked up stones to throw at him, but Jesus hid himself and went out of the temple.

Comments on Chapter 8

Ouch! Jesus touches a nerve. It's far easier to point out someone else's sin than it is to admit to your own. Jesus' mission is not to condemn guilty people, but to free people from guilt. Not only are we **dead in sins**, we're also **slaves to sin**. Only Jesus can make us truly free.

Think it through

1. Do you find it easier to point out someone else's sin than admit to your own?

2. Jesus says the religious leaders of the day would naturally believe lies instead of the truth. Do you think the reluctance we have in owning up to our own sin shows that we have the same tendency?

3. Jesus says, 'everyone who practises sin is a slave to sin' (v34). How have you seen the truth of this played out in your own life?

watch video clip

www.johnsgospel.org.uk/chapter8

Notes:

v51: Jesus is not referring to physical death, but spiritual death – eternal separation from God. Those who believe his words will have an eternal, permanent and living relationship with God in heaven.

Jesus Heals a Man Born Blind

9 As he passed by, he saw a man blind from birth. 2 And his disciples asked him, "Rabbi, who sinned, this man or his parents, that he was born blind?" 3 Jesus answered, "It was not that this man sinned, or his parents, but that the works of God might be displayed in him. 4 We must work the works of him who sent me while it is day; night is coming, when no one can work. 5 As long as I am in the world, I am the light of the world." 6 Having said these things, he spat on the ground and made mud with the saliva. Then he anointed the man's eyes with the mud 7 and said to him, "Go, wash in the pool of Siloam" (which means Sent). So he went and washed and came back seeing.

8 The neighbours and those who had seen him before as a beggar were saying, "Is this not the man who used to sit and beg?" 9 Some said, "It is he." Others said, "No, but he is like him." He kept saying, "I am the man." 10 So they said to him, "Then how were your eyes opened?" 11 He answered, "The man called Jesus made mud and anointed my eyes and said to me, 'Go to Siloam and wash.' So I went and washed and received my sight." 12 They said to him, "Where is he?" He said, "I do not know."

13 They brought to the Pharisees the man who had formerly been blind. 14 Now it was a Sabbath day when Jesus made the mud and opened his eyes. 15 So the Pharisees again asked him how he had received his sight. And he said to them, "He put mud on my eyes, and I washed, and I see." 16 Some of the Pharisees said, "This man is not from God, for he does not keep the Sabbath." But others said, "How can a man who is a sinner do such signs?" And there was a division among them. 17 So they said again to the blind man, "What do you say about him, since he has opened your eyes?" He said, "He is a prophet."

[18] The Jews did not believe that he had been blind and had received his sight, until they called the parents of the man who had received his sight [19] and asked them, "Is this your son, who you say was born blind? How then does he now see?" [20] His parents answered, "We know that this is our son and that he was born blind. [21] But how he now sees we do not know, nor do we know who opened his eyes. Ask him; he is of age. He will speak for himself." [22] (His parents said these things because they feared the Jews, for the Jews had already agreed that if anyone should confess Jesus to be Christ, he was to be put out of the synagogue.) [23] Therefore his parents said, "He is of age; ask him."

[24] So for the second time they called the man who had been blind and said to him, "Give glory to God. We know that this man is a sinner." [25] He answered, "Whether he is a sinner I do not know. One thing I do know, that though I was blind, now I see." [26] They said to him, "What did he do to you? How did he open your eyes?" [27] He answered them, "I have told you already, and you would not listen. Why do you want to hear it again? Do you also want to become his disciples?" [28] And they reviled him, saying, "You are his disciple, but we are disciples of Moses. [29] We know that God has spoken to Moses, but as for this man, we do not know where he comes from." [30] The man answered, "Why, this is an amazing thing! You do not know where he comes from, and yet he opened my eyes. [31] We know that God does not listen to sinners, but if anyone is a worshipper of God and does his will, God listens to him. [32] Never since the world began has it been heard that anyone opened the eyes of a man born blind. [33] If this man were not from God, he could do nothing." [34] They answered him, "You were born in utter sin, and would you teach us?" And they cast him out.

^{35} Jesus heard that they had cast him out, and having found him he said, "Do you believe in the Son of Man?" ^{36} He answered, "And who is he, sir, that I may believe in him?" ^{37} Jesus said to him, "You have seen him, and it is he who is speaking to you." ^{38} He said, "Lord, I believe", and he worshipped him. ^{39} Jesus said, "For judgement I came into this world, that those who do not see may see, and those who see may become blind." ^{40} Some of the Pharisees near him heard these things, and said to him, "Are we also blind?" ^{41} Jesus said to them, "If you were blind, you would have no guilt; but now that you say, 'We see', your guilt remains.

Comments on Chapter 9

'You can't possibly be the same man. You weren't born blind – you're lying, and an ignorant sinner!' Talk about open denial! The religious leaders are looking for every possible loophole to discredit the evidence of the man who can now see. The stakes are too high; if Jesus really has performed this miracle, it's positive proof that he is the sinless Son of God – and they know it. No wonder that, when all else fails, they resort to arrogant insults. Closed minds rarely acknowledge the truth, whereas the straightforward logical honesty of the blind man brings him to the truth. Who are the real blind people?!

Think it through

1. The man's parents don't want to voice any support for Jesus, for fear of the consequences. They prefer to remain neutral and sit on the fence. Are you ever tempted to do the same?

2. Does fear of others' opinions of you influence your own view of Jesus?
3. Is your opinion of Jesus negatively prejudiced and biased, or are you open-minded, willing to go where the evidence leads?

watch video clip
www.johnsgospel.org.uk/chapter9

I Am the Good Shepherd

10

"Truly, truly, I say to you, he who does not enter the sheepfold by the door but climbs in by another way, that man is a thief and a robber. ²But he who enters by the door is the shepherd of the sheep. ³To him the gatekeeper opens. The sheep hear his voice, and he calls his own sheep by name and leads them out. ⁴When he has brought out all his own, he goes before them, and the sheep follow him, for they know his voice. ⁵A stranger they will not follow, but they will flee from him, for they do not know the voice of strangers." ⁶This figure of speech Jesus used with them, but they did not understand what he was saying to them.

⁷So Jesus again said to them, "Truly, truly, I say to you, I am the door of the sheep. ⁸All who came before me are thieves and robbers, but the sheep did not listen to them. ⁹I am the door. If anyone enters by me, he will be saved and will go in and out and find pasture. ¹⁰The thief comes only to steal and kill and destroy. I came that they may have life and have it abundantly. ¹¹I am the good shepherd. The good shepherd lays down his life for the sheep. ¹²He who is a hired hand and not a shepherd, who does not own the sheep, sees the wolf coming and leaves the sheep and flees, and the wolf snatches them and scatters them. ¹³He flees because he is a hired hand and cares nothing for the sheep. ¹⁴I am the good shepherd. I know my own and my own know me, ¹⁵just as the Father knows me and I know the Father; and I lay down my life for the sheep. ¹⁶And I have other sheep that are not of this fold. I must bring them also, and they will listen to my voice. So there will be one flock, one shepherd. ¹⁷For this reason the Father loves me, because I lay down my life that I may take it up again. ¹⁸No one takes it from me, but I lay it down of my own accord. I have authority to lay it down, and I have

authority to take it up again. This charge I have received from my Father."

¹⁹ There was again a division among the Jews because of these words. ²⁰ Many of them said, "He has a demon, and is insane; why listen to him?" ²¹ Others said, "These are not the words of one who is oppressed by a demon. Can a demon open the eyes of the blind?"

I and the Father Are One

²² At that time the Feast of Dedication took place at Jerusalem. It was winter, ²³ and Jesus was walking in the temple, in the colonnade of Solomon. ²⁴ So the Jews gathered around him and said to him, "How long will you keep us in suspense? If you are the Christ, tell us plainly." ²⁵ Jesus answered them, "I told you, and you do not believe. The works that I do in my Father's name bear witness about me, ²⁶ but you do not believe because you are not among my sheep. ²⁷ My sheep hear my voice, and I know them, and they follow me. ²⁸ I give them eternal life, and they will never perish, and no one will snatch them out of my hand. ²⁹ My Father, who has given them to me, is greater than all, and no one is able to snatch them out of the Father's hand. ³⁰ I and the Father are one."

³¹ The Jews picked up stones again to stone him. ³² Jesus answered them, "I have shown you many good works from the Father; for which of them are you going to stone me?" ³³ The Jews answered him, "It is not for a good work that we are going to stone you but for blasphemy, because you, being a man, make yourself God." ³⁴ Jesus answered them, "Is it not written in your Law, 'I said, you are gods'? ³⁵ If he called them gods to whom the word of God came—and Scripture cannot be broken— ³⁶ do you say of him whom the Father consecrated and sent into the world, 'You are blaspheming', because I said, 'I am the

Son of God'? 37 If I am not doing the works of my Father, then do not believe me; 38 but if I do them, even though you do not believe me, believe the works, that you may know and understand that the Father is in me and I am in the Father." 39 Again they sought to arrest him, but he escaped from their hands.

40 He went away again across the Jordan to the place where John had been baptizing at first, and there he remained. 41 And many came to him. And they said, "John did no sign, but everything that John said about this man was true." 42 And many believed in him there.

Comments on Chapter 10

That's some love – a shepherd dying in order to save his sheep! Yet this is precisely what Jesus says he has come to do. And that's not the end of the story. Not only does Jesus say that he will willingly die, he also makes the incredible claim that he has the power to come back to life again (v17–18). This is no ordinary man!

Think it through

1. Verse 24 isn't a genuine question, the religious leaders are only looking for grounds on which to accuse Jesus of blasphemy. Have you ever made up your mind about Jesus before hearing all the facts?

2. The religious leaders are upset with Jesus claiming to be God (v33). Do you think he is blaspheming?

3. Jesus says that those to whom he gives eternal life are eternally safe (v28). How certain are you about where you will spend eternity?

4. Jesus says his mission is to give **abundant life** (v10). This implies that naturally we don't have it. Would you describe your current situation as life in abundance?

watch video clip
www.johnsgospel.org.uk/chapter10

The Death of Lazarus

11 Now a certain man was ill, Lazarus of Bethany, the village of Mary and her sister Martha. ² It was Mary who anointed the Lord with ointment and wiped his feet with her hair, whose brother Lazarus was ill. ³ So the sisters sent to him, saying, "Lord, he whom you love is ill." ⁴ But when Jesus heard it he said, "This illness does not lead to death. It is for the glory of God, so that the Son of God may be glorified through it."

⁵ Now Jesus loved Martha and her sister and Lazarus. ⁶ So, when he heard that Lazarus was ill, he stayed two days longer in the place where he was. ⁷ Then after this he said to the disciples, "Let us go to Judea again." ⁸ The disciples said to him, "Rabbi, the Jews were just now seeking to stone you, and are you going there again?" ⁹ Jesus answered, "Are there not twelve hours in the day? If anyone walks in the day, he does not stumble, because he sees the light of this world. ¹⁰ But if anyone walks in the night, he stumbles, because the light is not in him." ¹¹ After saying these things, he said to them, "Our friend Lazarus has fallen asleep, but I go to awaken him." ¹² The disciples said to him, "Lord, if he has fallen asleep, he will recover." ¹³ Now Jesus had spoken of his death, but they thought that he meant taking rest in sleep. ¹⁴ Then Jesus told them plainly, "Lazarus has died, ¹⁵ and for your sake I am glad that I was not there, so that you may believe. But let us go to him." ¹⁶ So Thomas, called the Twin, said to his fellow disciples, "Let us also go, that we may die with him."

I Am the Resurrection and the Life

¹⁷ Now when Jesus came, he found that Lazarus had already been in the tomb four days. ¹⁸ Bethany was near Jerusalem, about two miles off, ¹⁹ and many of the Jews

had come to Martha and Mary to console them concerning their brother. ²⁰ So when Martha heard that Jesus was coming, she went and met him, but Mary remained seated in the house. ²¹ Martha said to Jesus, "Lord, if you had been here, my brother would not have died. ²² But even now I know that whatever you ask from God, God will give you." ²³ Jesus said to her, "Your brother will rise again." ²⁴ Martha said to him, "I know that he will rise again in the resurrection on the last day." ²⁵ Jesus said to her, "I am the resurrection and the life. Whoever believes in me, though he die, yet shall he live, ²⁶ and everyone who lives and believes in me shall never die. Do you believe this?" ²⁷ She said to him, "Yes, Lord; I believe that you are the Christ, the Son of God, who is coming into the world."

Jesus Weeps

²⁸ When she had said this, she went and called her sister Mary, saying in private, "The Teacher is here and is calling for you." ²⁹ And when she heard it, she rose quickly and went to him. ³⁰ Now Jesus had not yet come into the village, but was still in the place where Martha had met him. ³¹ When the Jews who were with her in the house, consoling her, saw Mary rise quickly and go out, they followed her, supposing that she was going to the tomb to weep there. ³² Now when Mary came to where Jesus was and saw him, she fell at his feet, saying to him, "Lord, if you had been here, my brother would not have died." ³³ When Jesus saw her weeping, and the Jews who had come with her also weeping, he was deeply moved in his spirit and greatly troubled. ³⁴ And he said, "Where have you laid him?" They said to him, "Lord, come and see." ³⁵ Jesus wept. ³⁶ So the Jews said, "See how he loved him!" ³⁷ But some of them said, "Could not he who opened the eyes of the blind man also have kept this man from dying?"

Jesus Raises Lazarus

³⁸ Then Jesus, deeply moved again, came to the tomb. It was a cave, and a stone lay against it. ³⁹ Jesus said, "Take away the stone." Martha, the sister of the dead man, said to him, "Lord, by this time there will be an odour, for he has been dead four days." ⁴⁰ Jesus said to her, "Did I not tell you that if you believed you would see the glory of God?" ⁴¹ So they took away the stone. And Jesus lifted up his eyes and said, "Father, I thank you that you have heard me. ⁴² I knew that you always hear me, but I said this on account of the people standing around, that they may believe that you sent me." ⁴³ When he had said these things, he cried out with a loud voice, "Lazarus, come out." ⁴⁴ The man who had died came out, his hands and feet bound with linen strips, and his face wrapped with a cloth. Jesus said to them, "Unbind him, and let him go."

The Plot to Kill Jesus

⁴⁵ Many of the Jews therefore, who had come with Mary and had seen what he did, believed in him, ⁴⁶ but some of them went to the Pharisees and told them what Jesus had done. ⁴⁷ So the chief priests and the Pharisees gathered the council and said, "What are we to do? For this man performs many signs. ⁴⁸ If we let him go on like this, everyone will believe in him, and the Romans will come and take away both our place and our nation." ⁴⁹ But one of them, Caiaphas, who was high priest that year, said to them, "You know nothing at all. ⁵⁰ Nor do you understand that it is better for you that one man should die for the people, not that the whole nation should perish." ⁵¹ He did not say this of his own accord, but being high priest that year he prophesied that Jesus would die for the nation, ⁵² and not for the nation only, but also to gather into one the children of God who are scattered abroad. ⁵³ So from

that day on they made plans to put him to death.

⁵⁴ Jesus therefore no longer walked openly among the Jews, but went from there to the region near the wilderness, to a town called Ephraim, and there he stayed with the disciples.

⁵⁵ Now the Passover of the Jews was at hand, and many went up from the country to Jerusalem before the Passover to purify themselves. ⁵⁶ They were looking for Jesus and saying to one another as they stood in the temple, "What do you think? That he will not come to the feast at all?" ⁵⁷ Now the chief priests and the Pharisees had given orders that if anyone knew where he was, he should let them know, so that they might arrest him.

Comments on Chapter 11

Death is always a sad occasion. Even Jesus weeps. The sisters' sorrow is compounded by the knowledge that Jesus could have prevented their brother from dying, but hasn't – does he not care? Jesus on the other hand has something far more amazing in mind – to give **life** to a **dead** person! Can there now be any question as to his identity? And yet for those refusing to believe, it's the final straw – murder now captivates their thoughts. Isn't it strange that when Jesus gives life, they plan death?

Think it through

1. The evidence for Jesus raising Lazarus is so overwhelming, the religious leaders don't even try to refute it! What would it take for you to believe in him?

2. Speaking about Jesus, the high priest says it is better

for one man to die for everyone, rather than for everyone to die (v50). How does this resonate with what Jesus has already revealed about his mission?

watch video clip
www.johnsgospel.org.uk/chapter11

Mary Anoints Jesus at Bethany

12 Six days before the Passover, Jesus therefore came to Bethany, where Lazarus was, whom Jesus had raised from the dead. ² So they gave a dinner for him there. Martha served, and Lazarus was one of those reclining with him at table. ³ Mary therefore took a pound of expensive ointment made from pure nard, and anointed the feet of Jesus and wiped his feet with her hair. The house was filled with the fragrance of the perfume. ⁴ But Judas Iscariot, one of his disciples (he who was about to betray him), said, ⁵ "Why was this ointment not sold for three hundred denarii and given to the poor?" ⁶ He said this, not because he cared about the poor, but because he was a thief, and having charge of the money bag he used to help himself to what was put into it. ⁷ Jesus said, "Leave her alone, so that she may keep it for the day of my burial. ⁸ For the poor you always have with you, but you do not always have me."

The Plot to Kill Lazarus

⁹ When the large crowd of the Jews learned that Jesus was there, they came, not only on account of him but also to see Lazarus, whom he had raised from the dead. ¹⁰ So the chief priests made plans to put Lazarus to death as well, ¹¹ because on account of him many of the Jews were going away and believing in Jesus.

The Triumphal Entry

¹² The next day the large crowd that had come to the feast heard that Jesus was coming to Jerusalem. ¹³ So they took branches of palm trees and went out to meet him, crying out, "Hosanna! Blessed is he who comes in the name of the Lord, even the King of Israel!" ¹⁴ And Jesus found a young donkey and sat on it, just as it is written,

¹⁵ "Fear not, daughter of Zion;

behold, your king is coming,

sitting on a donkey's colt!"

¹⁶ His disciples did not understand these things at first, but when Jesus was glorified, then they remembered that these things had been written about him and had been done to him. ¹⁷ The crowd that had been with him when he called Lazarus out of the tomb and raised him from the dead continued to bear witness. ¹⁸ The reason why the crowd went to meet him was that they heard he had done this sign. ¹⁹ So the Pharisees said to one another, "You see that you are gaining nothing. Look, the world has gone after him."

Some Greeks Seek Jesus

²⁰ Now among those who went up to worship at the feast were some Greeks. ²¹ So these came to Philip, who was from Bethsaida in Galilee, and asked him, "Sir, we wish to see Jesus." ²² Philip went and told Andrew; Andrew and Philip went and told Jesus. ²³ And Jesus answered them, "The hour has come for the Son of Man to be glorified. ²⁴ Truly, truly, I say to you, unless a grain of wheat falls into the earth and dies, it remains alone; but if it dies, it bears much fruit. ²⁵ Whoever loves his life loses it, and whoever hates his life in this world will keep it for eternal life. ²⁶ If anyone serves me, he must follow me; and where I am, there will my servant be also. If anyone serves me, the Father will honour him.

The Son of Man Must Be Lifted Up

²⁷ "Now is my soul troubled. And what shall I say? 'Father, save me from this hour'? But for this purpose I have come to this hour. ²⁸ Father, glorify your name." Then

a voice came from heaven: "I have glorified it, and I will glorify it again." 29 The crowd that stood there and heard it said that it had thundered. Others said, "An angel has spoken to him." 30 Jesus answered, "This voice has come for your sake, not mine. 31 Now is the judgement of this world; now will the ruler of this world be cast out. 32 And I, when I am lifted up from the earth, will draw all people to myself." 33 He said this to show by what kind of death he was going to die. 34 So the crowd answered him, "We have heard from the Law that the Christ remains for ever. How can you say that the Son of Man must be lifted up? Who is this Son of Man?" 35 So Jesus said to them, "The light is among you for a little while longer. Walk while you have the light, lest darkness overtake you. The one who walks in the darkness does not know where he is going. 36 While you have the light, believe in the light, that you may become sons of light."

The Unbelief of the People

When Jesus had said these things, he departed and hid himself from them. 37 Though he had done so many signs before them, they still did not believe in him, 38 so that the word spoken by the prophet Isaiah might be fulfilled:

> "Lord, who has believed what he heard from us,
>   and to whom has the arm of the Lord been
>   revealed?"

39 Therefore they could not believe. For again Isaiah said,

40   "He has blinded their eyes
        and hardened their heart,

> lest they see with their eyes,
>> and understand with their heart, and turn,
>> and I would heal them."

[41] Isaiah said these things because he saw his glory and spoke of him. [42] Nevertheless, many even of the authorities believed in him, but for fear of the Pharisees they did not confess it, so that they would not be put out of the synagogue; [43] for they loved the glory that comes from man more than the glory that comes from God.

Jesus Came to Save the World

[44] And Jesus cried out and said, "Whoever believes in me, believes not in me but in him who sent me. [45] And whoever sees me sees him who sent me. [46] I have come into the world as light, so that whoever believes in me may not remain in darkness. [47] If anyone hears my words and does not keep them, I do not judge him; for I did not come to judge the world but to save the world. [48] The one who rejects me and does not receive my words has a judge; the word that I have spoken will judge him on the last day. [49] For I have not spoken on my own authority, but the Father who sent me has himself given me a commandment— what to say and what to speak. [50] And I know that his commandment is eternal life. What I say, therefore, I say as the Father has told me."

Comments on Chapter 12

Who is a real follower? Judas is a follower but not a believer, manipulating the situation for his own ends (v1–8). Some rulers are believers but not followers, unwilling to nail their colours to the mast and be associated with Jesus (v42–43). Neither believing nor following by itself is good enough – Jesus requires both. There is a cost in following Him, but the eternal rewards far outweigh the temporary loss. You can't be half-hearted about it – it's all or nothing.

Think it through

1. Jesus says a grain of wheat falling into the ground (effectively dying in order to produce more fruit) is a picture of what he has come to do. Through his death, you can have life. Why do you think he did it?

2. Some people are more concerned about what other people think of them than what God thinks of them (v42–43). This fear of other people stops them from following Jesus, even though they believe that what he says is true! What motives govern your actions? Are they stopping you from following Jesus?

watch video clip
www.johnsgospel.org.uk/chapter12

Jesus Washes the Disciples' Feet

13

Now before the Feast of the Passover, when Jesus knew that his hour had come to depart out of this world to the Father, having loved his own who were in the world, he loved them to the end. 2 During supper, when the devil had already put it into the heart of Judas Iscariot, Simon's son, to betray him, 3 Jesus, knowing that the Father had given all things into his hands, and that he had come from God and was going back to God, 4 rose from supper. He laid aside his outer garments, and taking a towel, tied it round his waist. 5 Then he poured water into a basin and began to wash the disciples' feet and to wipe them with the towel that was wrapped round him. 6 He came to Simon Peter, who said to him, "Lord, do you wash my feet?" 7 Jesus answered him, "What I am doing you do not understand now, but afterwards you will understand." 8 Peter said to him, "You shall never wash my feet." Jesus answered him, "If I do not wash you, you have no share with me." 9 Simon Peter said to him, "Lord, not my feet only but also my hands and my head!" 10 Jesus said to him, "The one who has bathed does not need to wash, except for his feet, but is completely clean. And you are clean, but not every one of you." 11 For he knew who was to betray him; that was why he said, "Not all of you are clean."

12 When he had washed their feet and put on his outer garments and resumed his place, he said to them, "Do you understand what I have done to you? 13 You call me Teacher and Lord, and you are right, for so I am. 14 If I then, your Lord and Teacher, have washed your feet, you also ought to wash one another's feet. 15 For I have given you an example, that you also should do just as I have done to you. 16 Truly, truly, I say to you, a servant is not greater than his master, nor is a messenger greater than the one who

sent him. [17] If you know these things, blessed are you if you do them. [18] I am not speaking of all of you; I know whom I have chosen. But the Scripture will be fulfilled, 'He who ate my bread has lifted his heel against me.' [19] I am telling you this now, before it takes place, that when it does take place you may believe that I am he. [20] Truly, truly, I say to you, whoever receives the one I send receives me, and whoever receives me receives the one who sent me."

One of You Will Betray Me

[21] After saying these things, Jesus was troubled in his spirit, and testified, "Truly, truly, I say to you, one of you will betray me." [22] The disciples looked at one another, uncertain of whom he spoke. [23] One of his disciples, whom Jesus loved, was reclining at table at Jesus' side, [24] so Simon Peter motioned to him to ask Jesus of whom he was speaking. [25] So that disciple, leaning back against Jesus, said to him, "Lord, who is it?" [26] Jesus answered, "It is he to whom I will give this morsel of bread when I have dipped it." So when he had dipped the morsel, he gave it to Judas, the son of Simon Iscariot. [27] Then after he had taken the morsel, Satan entered into him. Jesus said to him, "What you are going to do, do quickly." [28] Now no one at the table knew why he said this to him. [29] Some thought that, because Judas had the money bag, Jesus was telling him, "Buy what we need for the feast", or that he should give something to the poor. [30] So, after receiving the morsel of bread, he immediately went out. And it was night.

A New Commandment

[31] When he had gone out, Jesus said, "Now is the Son of Man glorified, and God is glorified in him. [32] If God is glorified in him, God will also glorify him in himself, and

glorify him at once. [33] Little children, yet a little while I am with you. You will seek me, and just as I said to the Jews, so now I also say to you, 'Where I am going you cannot come.' [34] A new commandment I give to you, that you love one another: just as I have loved you, you also are to love one another. [35] By this all people will know that you are my disciples, if you have love for one another."

Jesus Foretells Peter's Denial

[36] Simon Peter said to him, "Lord, where are you going?" Jesus answered him, "Where I am going you cannot follow me now, but you will follow afterwards." [37] Peter said to him, "Lord, why can I not follow you now? I will lay down my life for you." [38] Jesus answered, "Will you lay down your life for me? Truly, truly, I say to you, the cock will not crow till you have denied me three times.

Comments on Chapter 13

This is radical! Washing other people's feet – who wants to live like that?! We're all interested in going up the social ladder, but Jesus says that instead we should climb down, putting others' interests before our own – something he not only preaches, but practises too. If Jesus really is who he says he is, then his is the most staggering step down imaginable – God leaving heaven to become a servant to people! And all because he loves us and wants to bring us back into a relationship with himself.

Think it through

1. Jesus knows that his disciples aren't grasping everything, but that later they will be able to look back on it and it will all make sense (v7, v19). Are Jesus' life and mission making any sense to you yet?

2. Jesus says that although his disciples can't go with him to heaven just yet, they will later join him there (v36). Are you confident of going too? It is possible to be certain!

watch video clip
www.johnsgospel.org.uk/chapter13

I Am the Way, and the Truth, and the Life

14 "Let not your hearts be troubled. Believe in God; believe also in me. ² In my Father's house are many rooms. If it were not so, would I have told you that I go to prepare a place for you? ³ And if I go and prepare a place for you, I will come again and will take you to myself, that where I am you may be also. ⁴ And you know the way to where I am going." ⁵ Thomas said to him, "Lord, we do not know where you are going. How can we know the way?" ⁶ Jesus said to him, "I am the way, and the truth, and the life. No one comes to the Father except through me. ⁷ If you had known me, you would have known my Father also. From now on you do know him and have seen him."

⁸ Philip said to him, "Lord, show us the Father, and it is enough for us." ⁹ Jesus said to him, "Have I been with you so long, and you still do not know me, Philip? Whoever has seen me has seen the Father. How can you say, 'Show us the Father'? ¹⁰ Do you not believe that I am in the Father and the Father is in me? The words that I say to you I do not speak on my own authority, but the Father who dwells in me does his works. ¹¹ Believe me that I am in the Father and the Father is in me, or else believe on account of the works themselves.

¹² "Truly, truly, I say to you, whoever believes in me will also do the works that I do; and greater works than these will he do, because I am going to the Father. ¹³ Whatever you ask in my name, this I will do, that the Father may be glorified in the Son. ¹⁴ If you ask me for anything in my name, I will do it.

Jesus Promises the Holy Spirit

¹⁵ "If you love me, you will keep my commandments. ¹⁶ And I will ask the Father, and he will give you another

Helper, to be with you for ever, ¹⁷ even the Spirit of truth, whom the world cannot receive, because it neither sees him nor knows him. You know him, for he dwells with you and will be in you.

¹⁸ "I will not leave you as orphans; I will come to you. ¹⁹ Yet a little while and the world will see me no more, but you will see me. Because I live, you also will live. ²⁰ In that day you will know that I am in my Father, and you in me, and I in you. ²¹ Whoever has my commandments and keeps them, he it is who loves me. And he who loves me will be loved by my Father, and I will love him and manifest myself to him." ²² Judas (not Iscariot) said to him, "Lord, how is it that you will manifest yourself to us, and not to the world?" ²³ Jesus answered him, "If anyone loves me, he will keep my word, and my Father will love him, and we will come to him and make our home with him. ²⁴ Whoever does not love me does not keep my words. And the word that you hear is not mine but the Father's who sent me.

²⁵ "These things I have spoken to you while I am still with you. ²⁶ But the Helper, the Holy Spirit, whom the Father will send in my name, he will teach you all things and bring to your remembrance all that I have said to you. ²⁷ Peace I leave with you; my peace I give to you. Not as the world gives do I give to you. Let not your hearts be troubled, neither let them be afraid. ²⁸ You heard me say to you, 'I am going away, and I will come to you.' If you loved me, you would have rejoiced, because I am going to the Father, for the Father is greater than I. ²⁹ And now I have told you before it takes place, so that when it does take place you may believe. ³⁰ I will no longer talk much with you, for the ruler of this world is coming. He has no claim on me, ³¹ but I do as the Father has commanded me, so that the world may know that I love the Father. Rise, let us go from here.

Comments on Chapter 14

The **only** way? We might not have a problem with Jesus claiming to being the way, the truth and the life (v6), but to accept that he is the **only** way... well, that's harder to swallow! And yet if Jesus is God the Son, he has the authority to make this incredible statement. Are you still questioning whether it can be true? So are some of the disciples; but that's why Jesus does so many miracles, so as to leave them in no doubt as to his true identity (v11). There is no other possible explanation.

Think it through

1. Are you trying to gain acceptance with God in some way other than coming through Jesus?
2. Do you ever worry that if you become a true follower of Jesus, you won't be able to keep it up? If so, there's help at hand. When someone becomes a true Christian, God by his Holy Spirit comes and lives inside them, giving them the power to live as they should.

watch video clip
www.johnsgospel.org.uk/chapter14

Notes:

The Bible says we can never make ourselves 'good enough'; the only way is through trusting in Jesus who is completely sinless, and therefore can be more than 'good enough' on our behalf.

I Am the True Vine

15 "I am the true vine, and my Father is the vine dresser. ² Every branch in me that does not bear fruit he takes away, and every branch that does bear fruit he prunes, that it may bear more fruit. ³ Already you are clean because of the word that I have spoken to you. ⁴ Abide in me, and I in you. As the branch cannot bear fruit by itself, unless it abides in the vine, neither can you, unless you abide in me. ⁵ I am the vine; you are the branches. Whoever abides in me and I in him, he it is that bears much fruit, for apart from me you can do nothing. ⁶ If anyone does not abide in me he is thrown away like a branch and withers; and the branches are gathered, thrown into the fire, and burned. ⁷ If you abide in me, and my words abide in you, ask whatever you wish, and it will be done for you. ⁸ By this my Father is glorified, that you bear much fruit and so prove to be my disciples. ⁹ As the Father has loved me, so have I loved you. Abide in my love. ¹⁰ If you keep my commandments, you will abide in my love, just as I have kept my Father's commandments and abide in his love. ¹¹ These things I have spoken to you, that my joy may be in you, and that your joy may be full.

¹² "This is my commandment, that you love one another as I have loved you. ¹³ Greater love has no one than this, that someone lay down his life for his friends. ¹⁴ You are my friends if you do what I command you. ¹⁵ No longer do I call you servants, for the servant does not know what his master is doing; but I have called you friends, for all that I have heard from my Father I have made known to you. ¹⁶ You did not choose me, but I chose you and appointed you that you should go and bear fruit and that your fruit should abide, so that whatever you ask the Father in my name, he may give it to you. ¹⁷ These things I command you, so that you will love one another.

The Hatred of the World

[18] "If the world hates you, know that it has hated me before it hated you. [19] If you were of the world, the world would love you as its own; but because you are not of the world, but I chose you out of the world, therefore the world hates you. [20] Remember the word that I said to you: 'A servant is not greater than his master.' If they persecuted me, they will also persecute you. If they kept my word, they will also keep yours. [21] But all these things they will do to you on account of my name, because they do not know him who sent me. [22] If I had not come and spoken to them, they would not have been guilty of sin, but now they have no excuse for their sin. [23] Whoever hates me hates my Father also. [24] If I had not done among them the works that no one else did, they would not be guilty of sin, but now they have seen and hated both me and my Father. [25] But the word that is written in their Law must be fulfilled: 'They hated me without a cause.'

[26] "But when the Helper comes, whom I will send to you from the Father, the Spirit of truth, who proceeds from the Father, he will bear witness about me. [27] And you also will bear witness, because you have been with me from the beginning.

Comments on Chapter 15

Jesus is brutally honest: following him won't make you popular. The disciples are soon to learn that! If the masses reject Jesus, it only follows that they'll also reject his followers. But the crowds are now in the worst situation possible: Jesus has demonstrated that he really is God, that he alone can free them from their sin and give them eternal life, but they still reject it. They are now without excuse.

Think it through

1. Would you be willing to die for someone else? That's precisely what Jesus came to do!
2. Has your opinion of Jesus changed? If you reject him, do you agree that you are without excuse for your sin?

watch video clip

www.johnsgospel.org.uk/chapter15

16

"I have said all these things to you to keep you from falling away. 2 They will put you out of the synagogues. Indeed, the hour is coming when whoever kills you will think he is offering service to God. 3 And they will do these things because they have not known the Father, nor me. 4 But I have said these things to you, that when their hour comes you may remember that I told them to you.

The Work of the Holy Spirit

"I did not say these things to you from the beginning, because I was with you. 5 But now I am going to him who sent me, and none of you asks me, 'Where are you going?' 6 But because I have said these things to you, sorrow has filled your heart. 7 Nevertheless, I tell you the truth: it is to your advantage that I go away, for if I do not go away, the Helper will not come to you. But if I go, I will send him to you. 8 And when he comes, he will convict the world concerning sin and righteousness and judgement: 9 concerning sin, because they do not believe in me; 10 concerning righteousness, because I go to the Father, and you will see me no longer; 11 concerning judgement, because the ruler of this world is judged.

12 "I still have many things to say to you, but you cannot bear them now. 13 When the Spirit of truth comes, he will guide you into all the truth, for he will not speak on his own authority, but whatever he hears he will speak, and he will declare to you the things that are to come. 14 He will glorify me, for he will take what is mine and declare it to you. 15 All that the Father has is mine; therefore I said that he will take what is mine and declare it to you.

Your Sorrow Will Turn into Joy

16 "A little while, and you will see me no longer; and

again a little while, and you will see me." ¹⁷ So some of his disciples said to one another, "What is this that he says to us, 'A little while, and you will not see me, and again a little while, and you will see me'; and, 'because I am going to the Father'?" ¹⁸ So they were saying, "What does he mean by 'a little while'? We do not know what he is talking about." ¹⁹ Jesus knew that they wanted to ask him, so he said to them, "Is this what you are asking yourselves, what I meant by saying, 'A little while and you will not see me, and again a little while and you will see me'? ²⁰ Truly, truly, I say to you, you will weep and lament, but the world will rejoice. You will be sorrowful, but your sorrow will turn into joy. ²¹ When a woman is giving birth, she has sorrow because her hour has come, but when she has delivered the baby, she no longer remembers the anguish, for joy that a human being has been born into the world. ²² So also you have sorrow now, but I will see you again, and your hearts will rejoice, and no one will take your joy from you. ²³ In that day you will ask nothing of me. Truly, truly, I say to you, whatever you ask of the Father in my name, he will give it to you. ²⁴ Until now you have asked nothing in my name. Ask, and you will receive, that your joy may be full.

I Have Overcome the World

²⁵ "I have said these things to you in figures of speech. The hour is coming when I will no longer speak to you in figures of speech but will tell you plainly about the Father. ²⁶ In that day you will ask in my name, and I do not say to you that I will ask the Father on your behalf; ²⁷ for the Father himself loves you, because you have loved me and have believed that I came from God. ²⁸ I came from the Father and have come into the world, and now I am leaving the world and going to the Father."

²⁹ His disciples said, "Ah, now you are speaking plainly

and not using figurative speech! ³⁰ Now we know that you know all things and do not need anyone to question you; this is why we believe that you came from God." ³¹ Jesus answered them, "Do you now believe? ³² Behold, the hour is coming, indeed it has come, when you will be scattered, each to his own home, and will leave me alone. Yet I am not alone, for the Father is with me. ³³ I have said these things to you, that in me you may have peace. In the world you will have tribulation. But take heart; I have overcome the world."

Comments on Chapter 16

It's not for the faint-hearted! Things are going to get tough. Jesus alludes to his murder and tells the disciples that whilst they'll be distraught and questioning their faith, others will be delighted that they've finally got rid of Jesus (or so they suppose!). But the ending is not as you would predict, instead it's as Jesus predicts – He's going to come back to life (v22). Then who will be rejoicing? (Keep reading, this is where things get really exciting.)

Think it through

1. What do you think of the statement Jesus makes that not believing in him is a sin (v8–9)?
2. Do you think that being a follower of Jesus is just a crutch for the weak? Jesus says that someone may well experience more difficulties in life as a result of being a Christian (e.g. misunderstanding, ridicule or rejection), but that through it all, they will experience a peace and joy that only he can give.

Notes:

Jesus will be deserted by all his followers, yet he won't
be alone as God the Father will still be with him (v32).
The time is coming, though, when even the Father will
forsake him.

The High Priestly Prayer

17 When Jesus had spoken these words, he lifted up his eyes to heaven, and said, "Father, the hour has come; glorify your Son that the Son may glorify you, ² since you have given him authority over all flesh, to give eternal life to all whom you have given him. ³ And this is eternal life, that they know you the only true God, and Jesus Christ whom you have sent. ⁴ I glorified you on earth, having accomplished the work that you gave me to do. ⁵ And now, Father, glorify me in your own presence with the glory that I had with you before the world existed.

⁶ "I have manifested your name to the people whom you gave me out of the world. Yours they were, and you gave them to me, and they have kept your word. ⁷ Now they know that everything that you have given me is from you. ⁸ For I have given them the words that you gave me, and they have received them and have come to know in truth that I came from you; and they have believed that you sent me. ⁹ I am praying for them. I am not praying for the world but for those whom you have given me, for they are yours. ¹⁰ All mine are yours, and yours are mine, and I am glorified in them. ¹¹ And I am no longer in the world, but they are in the world, and I am coming to you. Holy Father, keep them in your name, which you have given me, that they may be one, even as we are one. ¹² While I was with them, I kept them in your name, which you have given me. I have guarded them, and not one of them has been lost except the son of destruction, that the Scripture might be fulfilled. ¹³ But now I am coming to you, and these things I speak in the world, that they may have my joy fulfilled in themselves. ¹⁴ I have given them your word, and the world has hated them because they are not of the world, just as I am not of the world. ¹⁵ I do not ask that you take them

out of the world, but that you keep them from the evil one. ¹⁶ They are not of the world, just as I am not of the world. ¹⁷ Sanctify them in the truth; your word is truth. ¹⁸ As you sent me into the world, so I have sent them into the world. ¹⁹ And for their sake I consecrate myself, that they also may be sanctified in truth.

²⁰ "I do not ask for these only, but also for those who will believe in me through their word, ²¹ that they may all be one, just as you, Father, are in me, and I in you, that they also may be in us, so that the world may believe that you have sent me. ²² The glory that you have given me I have given to them, that they may be one even as we are one, ²³ I in them and you in me, that they may become perfectly one, so that the world may know that you sent me and loved them even as you loved me. ²⁴ Father, I desire that they also, whom you have given me, may be with me where I am, to see my glory that you have given me because you loved me before the foundation of the world. ²⁵ O righteous Father, even though the world does not know you, I know you, and these know that you have sent me. ²⁶ I made known to them your name, and I will continue to make it known, that the love with which you have loved me may be in them, and I in them."

Comments on Chapter 17

What a privilege – to hear Jesus speaking to his Father. But eternal life – what's that about? No one on this earth lives forever! But Jesus speaks a lot about it, so what does he mean? He's talking about what happens to the real you after your body dies. Knowing the 'only true God' in a personal way through Jesus means that we'll be able to live with him forever (v3). For those that reject him, the alternative is terrible. Jesus cares; he cares about your eternal destiny – that's why he came. He wants the amazing love between God the Father and God the Son to be extended to include you!

Think it through

1. Accepting God's word to be true and following it could result in opposition. Do you think eternal life is worth it?
2. Jesus speaks about a true love and unity that can only be found through him. So often in life we see the complete opposite being played out in people's lives. Why do you think this is?

watch video clip
www.johnsgospel.org.uk/chapter17

Betrayal and Arrest of Jesus

18 When Jesus had spoken these words, he went out with his disciples across the brook Kidron, where there was a garden, which he and his disciples entered. ² Now Judas, who betrayed him, also knew the place, for Jesus often met there with his disciples. ³ So Judas, having procured a band of soldiers and some officers from the chief priests and the Pharisees, went there with lanterns and torches and weapons. ⁴ Then Jesus, knowing all that would happen to him, came forward and said to them, "Whom do you seek?" ⁵ They answered him, "Jesus of Nazareth." Jesus said to them, "I am he." Judas, who betrayed him, was standing with them. ⁶ When Jesus said to them, "I am he", they drew back and fell to the ground. ⁷ So he asked them again, "Whom do you seek?" And they said, "Jesus of Nazareth." ⁸ Jesus answered, "I told you that I am he. So, if you seek me, let these men go." ⁹ This was to fulfil the word that he had spoken: "Of those whom you gave me I have lost not one." ¹⁰ Then Simon Peter, having a sword, drew it and struck the high priest's servant and cut off his right ear. (The servant's name was Malchus.) ¹¹ So Jesus said to Peter, "Put your sword into its sheath; shall I not drink the cup that the Father has given me?"

Jesus Faces Annas and Caiaphas

¹² So the band of soldiers and their captain and the officers of the Jews arrested Jesus and bound him. ¹³ First they led him to Annas, for he was the father-in-law of Caiaphas, who was high priest that year. ¹⁴ It was Caiaphas who had advised the Jews that it would be expedient that one man should die for the people.

Peter Denies Jesus

¹⁵ Simon Peter followed Jesus, and so did another disciple. Since that disciple was known to the high priest, he entered with Jesus into the courtyard of the high priest, ¹⁶ but Peter stood outside at the door. So the other disciple, who was known to the high priest, went out and spoke to the servant girl who kept watch at the door, and brought Peter in. ¹⁷ The servant girl at the door said to Peter, "You also are not one of this man's disciples, are you?" He said, "I am not." ¹⁸ Now the servants and officers had made a charcoal fire, because it was cold, and they were standing and warming themselves. Peter also was with them, standing and warming himself.

The High Priest Questions Jesus

¹⁹ The high priest then questioned Jesus about his disciples and his teaching. ²⁰ Jesus answered him, "I have spoken openly to the world. I have always taught in synagogues and in the temple, where all Jews come together. I have said nothing in secret. ²¹ Why do you ask me? Ask those who have heard me what I said to them; they know what I said." ²² When he had said these things, one of the officers standing by struck Jesus with his hand, saying, "Is that how you answer the high priest?" ²³ Jesus answered him, "If what I said is wrong, bear witness about the wrong; but if what I said is right, why do you strike me?" ²⁴ Annas then sent him bound to Caiaphas the high priest.

Peter Denies Jesus Again

²⁵ Now Simon Peter was standing and warming himself. So they said to him, "You also are not one of his disciples, are you?" He denied it and said, "I am not." ²⁶ One of the servants of the high priest, a relative of the man whose

ear Peter had cut off, asked, "Did I not see you in the garden with him?" ²⁷ Peter again denied it, and at once a cock crowed.

Jesus Before Pilate

²⁸ Then they led Jesus from the house of Caiaphas to the governor's headquarters. It was early morning. They themselves did not enter the governor's headquarters, so that they would not be defiled, but could eat the Passover. ²⁹ So Pilate went outside to them and said, "What accusation do you bring against this man?" ³⁰ They answered him, "If this man were not doing evil, we would not have delivered him over to you." ³¹ Pilate said to them, "Take him yourselves and judge him by your own law." The Jews said to him, "It is not lawful for us to put anyone to death." ³² This was to fulfil the word that Jesus had spoken to show by what kind of death he was going to die.

My Kingdom Is Not of This World

³³ So Pilate entered his headquarters again and called Jesus and said to him, "Are you the King of the Jews?" ³⁴ Jesus answered, "Do you say this of your own accord, or did others say it to you about me?" ³⁵ Pilate answered, "Am I a Jew? Your own nation and the chief priests have delivered you over to me. What have you done?" ³⁶ Jesus answered, "My kingdom is not of this world. If my kingdom were of this world, my servants would have been fighting, that I might not be delivered over to the Jews. But my kingdom is not from the world." ³⁷ Then Pilate said to him, "So you are a king?" Jesus answered, "You say that I am a king. For this purpose I was born and for this purpose I have come into the world—to bear witness to the truth. Everyone who is of the truth listens to my voice." ³⁸ Pilate said to him, "What is truth?"

After he had said this, he went back outside to the Jews and told them, "I find no guilt in him. ³⁹ But you have a custom that I should release one man for you at the Passover. So do you want me to release to you the King of the Jews?" ⁴⁰ They cried out again, "Not this man, but Barabbas!" Now Barabbas was a robber.

Comments on Chapter 18

'What is truth?' That's a good question. Solve this one and you've got it nailed! Many claim there is no definitive answer, but Jesus makes the bold statement that truth is what he's all about. He came to show the truth; he is the **truth** (ch14 v6). Like so many today, Pilate asks the question but doesn't really want to discover the answer. It's an easy question to hide behind if you don't want to face the truth – because sometimes the truth hurts! The test of whether you are genuinely seeking the truth is if you are willing to go wherever the evidence leads, even if it's inconvenient to you.

Think it through

1. This is it; they're out to kill him. But Jesus doesn't run, he doesn't hide – this is what he's come for! It might seem strange, but can you see how this is fulfilling his mission? (Clue: see ch10 v11 – the good shepherd giving his life for the sheep.)
2. Do you think Jesus is worthy of death? What crime are they accusing him of? (Pilate couldn't figure it out either!)

3. Jesus says he's a king. Are you willing to bow before him?

watch video clip
www.johnsgospel.org.uk/chapter18

Jesus Delivered to Be Crucified

19 Then Pilate took Jesus and flogged him. ²And the soldiers twisted together a crown of thorns and put it on his head and arrayed him in a purple robe. ³They came up to him, saying, "Hail, King of the Jews!" and struck him with their hands. ⁴Pilate went out again and said to them, "See, I am bringing him out to you that you may know that I find no guilt in him." ⁵So Jesus came out, wearing the crown of thorns and the purple robe. Pilate said to them, "Behold the man!" ⁶When the chief priests and the officers saw him, they cried out, "Crucify him, crucify him!" Pilate said to them, "Take him yourselves and crucify him, for I find no guilt in him." ⁷The Jews answered him, "We have a law, and according to that law he ought to die because he has made himself the Son of God." ⁸When Pilate heard this statement, he was even more afraid. ⁹He entered his headquarters again and said to Jesus, "Where are you from?" But Jesus gave him no answer. ¹⁰So Pilate said to him, "You will not speak to me? Do you not know that I have authority to release you and authority to crucify you?" ¹¹Jesus answered him, "You would have no authority over me at all unless it had been given you from above. Therefore he who delivered me over to you has the greater sin."

¹²From then on Pilate sought to release him, but the Jews cried out, "If you release this man, you are not Caesar's friend. Everyone who makes himself a king opposes Caesar." ¹³So when Pilate heard these words, he brought Jesus out and sat down on the judgement seat at a place called The Stone Pavement, and in Aramaic Gabbatha. ¹⁴Now it was the day of Preparation of the Passover. It was about the sixth hour. He said to the Jews, "Behold your King!" ¹⁵They cried out, "Away with him, away with him, crucify him!" Pilate said to them, "Shall I

crucify your King?" The chief priests answered, "We have no king but Caesar." ¹⁶ So he delivered him over to them to be crucified.

The Crucifixion

So they took Jesus, ¹⁷ and he went out, bearing his own cross, to the place called The Place of a Skull, which in Aramaic is called Golgotha. ¹⁸ There they crucified him, and with him two others, one on either side, and Jesus between them. ¹⁹ Pilate also wrote an inscription and put it on the cross. It read, "Jesus of Nazareth, the King of the Jews." ²⁰ Many of the Jews read this inscription, for the place where Jesus was crucified was near the city, and it was written in Aramaic, in Latin, and in Greek. ²¹ So the chief priests of the Jews said to Pilate, "Do not write, 'The King of the Jews', but rather, 'This man said, I am King of the Jews.'" ²² Pilate answered, "What I have written I have written."

²³ When the soldiers had crucified Jesus, they took his garments and divided them into four parts, one part for each soldier; also his tunic. But the tunic was seamless, woven in one piece from top to bottom, ²⁴ so they said to one another, "Let us not tear it, but cast lots for it to see whose it shall be." This was to fulfil the Scripture which says,

"They divided my garments among them,
    and for my clothing they cast lots."

So the soldiers did these things, ²⁵ but standing by the cross of Jesus were his mother and his mother's sister, Mary the wife of Clopas, and Mary Magdalene. ²⁶ When Jesus saw his mother and the disciple whom he loved standing nearby, he said to his mother, "Woman, behold, your son!" 27 Then he said to the disciple, "Behold, your mother!" And from that hour the disciple took her to his own home.

The Death of Jesus

28 After this, Jesus, knowing that all was now finished, said (to fulfil the Scripture), "I thirst." 29 A jar full of sour wine stood there, so they put a sponge full of the sour wine on a hyssop branch and held it to his mouth. 30 When Jesus had received the sour wine, he said, "It is finished", and he bowed his head and gave up his spirit.

Jesus' Side Is Pierced

31 Since it was the day of Preparation, and so that the bodies would not remain on the cross on the Sabbath (for that Sabbath was a high day), the Jews asked Pilate that their legs might be broken and that they might be taken away. 32 So the soldiers came and broke the legs of the first, and of the other who had been crucified with him. 33 But when they came to Jesus and saw that he was already dead, they did not break his legs. 34 But one of the soldiers pierced his side with a spear, and at once there came out blood and water. 35 He who saw it has borne witness—his testimony is true, and he knows that he is telling the truth—that you also may believe. 36 For these things took place that the Scripture might be fulfilled: "Not one of his bones will be broken." 37 And again another Scripture says, "They will look on him whom they have pierced."

Jesus Is Buried

38 After these things Joseph of Arimathea, who was a disciple of Jesus, but secretly for fear of the Jews, asked Pilate that he might take away the body of Jesus, and

Pilate gave him permission. So he came and took away his body. ³⁹ Nicodemus also, who earlier had come to Jesus by night, came bringing a mixture of myrrh and aloes, about seventy-five pounds in weight. ⁴⁰ So they took the body of Jesus and bound it in linen cloths with the spices, as is the burial custom of the Jews. ⁴¹ Now in the place where he was crucified there was a garden, and in the garden a new tomb in which no one had yet been laid. ⁴² So because of the Jewish day of Preparation, since the tomb was close at hand, they laid Jesus there.

Comments on Chapter 19

What an incredible travesty of justice! Jesus is crucified because the religious leaders can't accept that he is God (v7). Three times Pilate states, 'I find no guilt in him.' But belief is different to action. He's afraid of God (v7–8), but he's afraid of people more! The fact that he believes Jesus to be innocent but refuses to act, in order to protect his own reputation, only makes him the guiltier! You wouldn't do the same… would you?

And so Jesus dies… but it's not over yet!

Think it through

1. Do you agree with Pilate that Jesus is innocent?
2. Men who were previously too afraid to follow Jesus now publicly nail their colours to the mast by burying his body. Is fear of others still holding you back from following Jesus?
3. This account is written by an eyewitness with the

purpose that you might believe (v35). Do you have any reason to doubt the account?

watch video clip
www.johnsgospel.org.uk/chapter19

Notes:

All through his life, Jesus fulfils prophecies that were made about him hundreds of years before he was born. They are too many and too detailed for their fulfilment to be pure coincidence! Many of them are outside Jesus' control, such as the soldiers casting lots for his garments whilst he's hanging on the cross (v24), or none of his bones being broken after he's died (v36).

The Resurrection

20 Now on the first day of the week Mary Magdalene came to the tomb early, while it was still dark, and saw that the stone had been taken away from the tomb. ² So she ran and went to Simon Peter and the other disciple, the one whom Jesus loved, and said to them, "They have taken the Lord out of the tomb, and we do not know where they have laid him." ³ So Peter went out with the other disciple, and they were going towards the tomb. ⁴ Both of them were running together, but the other disciple outran Peter and reached the tomb first. ⁵ And stooping to look in, he saw the linen cloths lying there, but he did not go in. ⁶ Then Simon Peter came, following him, and went into the tomb. He saw the linen cloths lying there, ⁷ and the face cloth, which had been on Jesus' head, not lying with the linen cloths but folded up in a place by itself. ⁸ Then the other disciple, who had reached the tomb first, also went in, and he saw and believed; ⁹ for as yet they did not understand the Scripture, that he must rise from the dead. ¹⁰ Then the disciples went back to their homes.

Jesus Appears to Mary Magdalene

¹¹ But Mary stood weeping outside the tomb, and as she wept she stooped to look into the tomb. ¹² And she saw two angels in white, sitting where the body of Jesus had lain, one at the head and one at the feet. ¹³ They said to her, "Woman, why are you weeping?" She said to them, "They have taken away my Lord, and I do not know where they have laid him." ¹⁴ Having said this, she turned round and saw Jesus standing, but she did not know that it was Jesus. ¹⁵ Jesus said to her, "Woman, why are you weeping? Whom are you seeking?" Supposing him to be the gardener, she said to him, "Sir, if you have carried him

away, tell me where you have laid him, and I will take him away." [16] Jesus said to her, "Mary." She turned and said to him in Aramaic, "Rabboni!" (which means Teacher). [17] Jesus said to her, "Do not cling to me, for I have not yet ascended to the Father; but go to my brothers and say to them, 'I am ascending to my Father and your Father, to my God and your God.'" [18] Mary Magdalene went and announced to the disciples, "I have seen the Lord"—and that he had said these things to her.

Jesus Appears to the Disciples

[19] On the evening of that day, the first day of the week, the doors being locked where the disciples were for fear of the Jews, Jesus came and stood among them and said to them, "Peace be with you." [20] When he had said this, he showed them his hands and his side. Then the disciples were glad when they saw the Lord. [21] Jesus said to them again, "Peace be with you. As the Father has sent me, even so I am sending you." [22] And when he had said this, he breathed on them and said to them, "Receive the Holy Spirit. [23] If you forgive the sins of any, they are forgiven them; if you withhold forgiveness from any, it is withheld."

Jesus and Thomas

[24] Now Thomas, one of the Twelve, called the Twin, was not with them when Jesus came. [25] So the other disciples told him, "We have seen the Lord." But he said to them, "Unless I see in his hands the mark of the nails, and place my finger into the mark of the nails, and place my hand into his side, I will never believe."

[26] Eight days later, his disciples were inside again, and Thomas was with them. Although the doors were locked, Jesus came and stood among them and said, "Peace be with you." [27] Then he said to Thomas, "Put your

finger here, and see my hands; and put out your hand, and place it in my side. Do not disbelieve, but believe." [28] Thomas answered him, "My Lord and my God!" [29] Jesus said to him, "Have you believed because you have seen me? Blessed are those who have not seen and yet have believed."

The Purpose of This Book

[30] Now Jesus did many other signs in the presence of the disciples, which are not written in this book; [31] but these are written so that you may believe that Jesus is the Christ, the Son of God, and that by believing you may have life in his name.

Comments on Chapter 20

Jesus is alive! Yes, even his disciples find it hard to believe at first – especially Thomas. He isn't going to believe a fairytale, he wants hard evidence – and he gets it! Faith in Jesus isn't a blind leap in the dark; it's a case of trusting reliable evidence. We can't see Jesus' wounds like Thomas does, but then that's why this book was written, so that you might believe the evidence, and in believing his true identity and sacrificial mission, you might have **life** (v31).

Think it through

1. What do you think to the statement that faith in Jesus is not a blind leap in the dark?

2. It's often said, '**seeing is believing**', but do you ever

believe without seeing? What do you make of all the evidence?

watch video clip
www.johnsgospel.org.uk/chapter20

Jesus Appears to Seven Disciples

21 After this Jesus revealed himself again to the disciples by the Sea of Tiberias, and he revealed himself in this way. ²Simon Peter, Thomas (called the Twin), Nathanael of Cana in Galilee, the sons of Zebedee, and two others of his disciples were together. ³Simon Peter said to them, "I am going fishing." They said to him, "We will go with you." They went out and got into the boat, but that night they caught nothing.

⁴Just as day was breaking, Jesus stood on the shore; yet the disciples did not know that it was Jesus. ⁵Jesus said to them, "Children, do you have any fish?" They answered him, "No." ⁶He said to them, "Cast the net on the right side of the boat, and you will find some." So they cast it, and now they were not able to haul it in, because of the quantity of fish. ⁷That disciple whom Jesus loved therefore said to Peter, "It is the Lord!" When Simon Peter heard that it was the Lord, he put on his outer garment, for he was stripped for work, and threw himself into the sea. ⁸The other disciples came in the boat, dragging the net full of fish, for they were not far from the land, but about a hundred yards off.

⁹When they got out on land, they saw a charcoal fire in place, with fish laid out on it, and bread. ¹⁰Jesus said to them, "Bring some of the fish that you have just caught." ¹¹So Simon Peter went aboard and hauled the net ashore, full of large fish, 153 of them. And although there were so many, the net was not torn. ¹²Jesus said to them, "Come and have breakfast." Now none of the disciples dared ask him, "Who are you?" They knew it was the Lord. ¹³Jesus came and took the bread and gave it to them, and so with the fish. ¹⁴This was now the third time that Jesus was revealed to the disciples after he was raised from the dead.

Jesus and Peter

15 When they had finished breakfast, Jesus said to Simon Peter, "Simon, son of John, do you love me more than these?" He said to him, "Yes, Lord; you know that I love you." He said to him, "Feed my lambs." 16 He said to him a second time, "Simon, son of John, do you love me?" He said to him, "Yes, Lord; you know that I love you." He said to him, "Tend my sheep." 17 He said to him the third time, "Simon, son of John, do you love me?" Peter was grieved because he said to him the third time, "Do you love me?" and he said to him, "Lord, you know everything; you know that I love you." Jesus said to him, "Feed my sheep. 18 Truly, truly, I say to you, when you were young, you used to dress yourself and walk wherever you wanted, but when you are old, you will stretch out your hands, and another will dress you and carry you where you do not want to go." 19 (This he said to show by what kind of death he was to glorify God.) And after saying this he said to him, "Follow me."

Jesus and the Beloved Apostle

20 Peter turned and saw the disciple whom Jesus loved following them, the one who also had leaned back against him during the supper and had said, "Lord, who is it that is going to betray you?" 21 When Peter saw him, he said to Jesus, "Lord, what about this man?" 22 Jesus said to him, "If it is my will that he remain until I come, what is that to you? You follow me!" 23 So the saying spread abroad among the brothers that this disciple was not to die; yet Jesus did not say to him that he was not to die, but, "If it is my will that he remain until I come, what is that to you?"

24 This is the disciple who is bearing witness about these things, and who has written these things, and we know that his testimony is true.

²⁵ Now there are also many other things that Jesus did. Were every one of them to be written, I suppose that the world itself could not contain the books that would be written.

Comments on Chapter 21

How could Peter now not love Jesus? Three times he utterly denied any connection to Jesus and swore he wasn't a follower of him. But Jesus forgives Peter and restores their relationship! This is what Jesus is all about: forgiveness. That's why he died on the cross, so that he could take the punishment himself that our sin deserves and restore our relationship with God. How could you not love Jesus for doing that?

Think it through

1. Are you thankful that Jesus died to take the punishment for your wrongdoing so that you can be forgiven?
2. Are you genuinely sorry for your sin and how it grieves God? Do you have a heartfelt desire to stop doing these things? Have you ever asked him to forgive you and change you?
3. Do you have a real living relationship with God?

watch video clip

www.johnsgospel.org.uk/chapter21

How will you respond to Jesus?

John's record leaves no question as to who Jesus really is. He is God! (See ch1, v1 and v14.) Neither does it leave any doubt as to why he came. Jesus said, 'I came that they may have life and have it abundantly' (ch10 v10).

This isn't just a nice biography about someone who lived 2000 years ago. These truths are dynamite! How you respond to them will have an eternal impact. You must get it right.

The big problem

However, not all truths are easy to swallow. One of the hardest is that you have a big problem: your sin. To many people, the idea of sin is offensive, but sin is doing anything that God, in his love, commands us not to. It's a deliberate flouting of his laws and living our own way. Sinning is easy. It comes naturally. But our sin has shattered our relationship with God. It is offensive to him and he can't just ignore it and sit idly by. His commands, which reflect his perfect character, have been violated. Sin must be punished – his justice requires it. The penalty is death – eternal separation from God.

It's not comfortable being told we're sinners who must be punished, and so our immediate response is often to justify ourselves. 'Why should we worry about what Jesus says anyway?' we ask. We're tempted to do the very worst thing possible – ignore and reject him. When we do this, we fulfil Jesus' prediction: 'this is the judgement: the light has come into the world, and people loved the darkness rather than the light because their works were evil' (ch3 v19).

The shadow of judgement looms over our heads. We *must* and *will* pay the consequences.

The only answer

Yet John's record of Jesus also offers hope. Despite all your sin, God loves you! He doesn't take delight in punishment, but he wants to restore your relationship with him. So he set about making it possible for you to be forgiven, with all your sin permanently taken away, so you can have eternal life with him in heaven.

However, God can't just ignore sin and brush it under the carpet – it must still be paid for. This is why Jesus came. You don't have to be the one who pays for it. Jesus offers to!

watch video clip
www.johnsgospel.org.uk/the-real-jesus

Jesus had no sin of his own to pay for, as he was sinless. Yet out of love, he willingly stood in and took the full weight of God's judgement against our sin. He personally bore the penalty. He died! He fully paid the price and three days later he rose from the dead. Sin had been paid for, death had been defeated, Jesus was victorious.

The offer of forgiveness is open to everyone. When the offer is accepted, an amazing transaction takes place.

Jesus takes our sin and all its consequences. In exchange, he gives us his perfection and all its eternal rewards.

Jesus said, 'For God so loved the world, that he gave his only Son, that whoever believes in him should not perish but have eternal life' (ch3 v16).

So, what about you?

As with all gifts, this offer is not yours until you *personally* accept it. Just because Jesus died, it doesn't mean everyone is automatically forgiven. Neither is it just a free ticket to heaven, meaning you can live your life as you like. God requires you to truly repent of your sin. This means having a genuine heartfelt sorrow for grieving him, unconditionally renouncing all your sin and wanting to live to please him. It means walking a new way: God's way. He must have his rightful place in your life; he must come first.

Does all this seem too much for you to keep up? Well, you're right – by yourself you can't do it. But you won't be on your own. God promises to be with you every step of the way. He will change your desires, values and priorities *from the inside*.

And so it is possible for *you* to be forgiven. For *you* to have your relationship with God restored and have eternal life! The offer is there – will you accept it? Have you ever thanked Jesus for dying in your place, turned from your sin, and asked him to forgive you and take control of your life? It's the only way to escape eternal death and enjoy *eternal life*. It's the biggest decision of your life. How will you respond?

'You will know the truth, and the truth will set you free' (ch8 v32).

Want to find out more about Christianity?

If you would like to know more about what it means to be a real Christian or would like more free resources to help you:

Visit:
www.johnsgospel.org.uk
www.thechristiananswer.org

Email:
info@johnsgospel.org.uk

Find out more.
www.johnsgospel.org.uk/find-out-more